COMPUTERS AND SOCIETY

COMPUTERS AND SOCIETY

Edited by
Colin Beardon and Diane Whitehouse

intellect
OXFORD, ENGLAND

First Published in 1993 by
Intellect Books
Suite 2, 108/110 London Road, Oxford OX3 9AW

Consulting editor:	Masoud Yazdani
Copy editor:	Cate Foster
Cover illustration:	Stuart Mealing
Typesetting:	Andrew Healey

British Library Cataloguing in Publication Data available

ISBN 1-871516-41-2

Printed and bound in Great Britain by Cromwell Press, Wiltshire

Contents

Contributors

Chrisanthi Avgerou, Department of Information Systems, London School of Economics, University of London, London WC2A 2AE, UK.
Chrisanthi Avgerou is a lecturer in Information Systems at the London School of Economics. Prior to that she worked as a programmer and systems analyst, developing banking systems. Her research interests include the relationship of information systems to institutional reform in the public sector, and the role of information technology in socio-economic development.

Colin Beardon, Rediffusion Simulation Research Centre, Faculty of Art, Design & Humanities, University of Brighton, Brighton BN2 2JY, UK.
Colin Beardon has both worked in the computer industry and has taught in higher education in the UK, Australia and New Zealand. He has published widely on the social effects of computerisation and on artificial intelligence and natural language processing. He is currently working in the area of multimedia computing and is Reader in Computer Graphics at the University of Brighton.

Jacques Berleur, Facultés Universitaires Notre-Dame de la Paix, Rue be Bruxelles 61, B-5000, Namur, Belgium.
Professor Jacques Berleur is presently Professor at the Institut d'Informatique of the Facultes Universitaires Notre-Dame de la Paix in Namur (Belgium). Engineer and philosopher, he is directing an interfaculty research unit on Technology Assessment (CITA) developing a systematic reflection on the social, economic, political and cultural impacts of computers on individuals and on society and an assessment of Information and Communication Technology. He is editor of a quarterly "Journal de Reflexion sur l'Informatique". He was, in 1976, a co-founder of IFIP-TC9 (Computers and Society) and has been its Belgian Representative since the beginning. Since 1990 he has been Chairman of IFIP-WG9.2 (Social Accountability). He is author or editor of some 10 books and author of more than 100 papers mainly in the field of Computers and Society. He has been Dean of the Institut d'Informatique (1979-84) and Rector of the University (1984-1993).

Gunilla Bradley, Institute of International Education, Stockholm University, S-10691 Stockholm, Sweden.
Gunilla Bradley is professor at the Institute of International Education, Stockholm University. She has published 9 books, including *Computers and the Psychosocial Work Environment* and *The Role of Engineers and the Future*

Computer Technology. She was awarded the "Golden Leaf" for important contributions within research on the psychosocial work environment and was elected Professional Woman of the Year in Sweden in 1989. In 1991 she was a visiting scholar at Stanford University, where she completed a 3-year project on Knowledge Based Systems and their Organisational and Psychosocial impact. Currently she is setting up a new research programme on "Human Communication - Psychosocial perspective on the Individual and the Society in Change" financed by The Bank of Sweden Tercentenary Foundation.

Geoff Busby, GEC-Marconi Research Centre, West Hanningfield Road, Great Baddow, Chelmsford, CM2 8HN, UK
Geoff Busby is disabled from birth with cerebral palsy. He has an MA in Computers and Psychology and has worked in the computer industry for more that 20 years. He is chairman of the British Computer Society Disabled Specialist Group and was a founder member of the Group in 1975. Geoff was director of a British Computer Society 'employment and disability' project from 1988-91. He is presently Chief Executive of the charity Compaid Trust, which advises on and teaches computer technology to people with disabilities. He is also an associate consultant for The Computability Centre, project leader of CEPIS (Council for Professional Informatics Society) Social Issues Task Force on Disability, and is responsible for disability issues within IFIP WG9.2. Geoff has travelled widely and presented papers on the subject of computers and disability in Europe, America, Japan, Scandinavia and Iraq. He was awarded an MBE for his work in 1992 and received the honorary degree of D.Univ from the University of Middlesex.

Simone Fischer-Hübner, Fachbereich Informatik, Vogt-Köln-Str. 30, 2000 Hamburg 54, Germany.
e-mail: fischer@rz.informatik.uni-hamburg.dbp.de
Simone Fischer-Hübner was born in Lübeck, Germany, on 13 January, 1963. She studied Computer Science with a minor in Law at the University of Hamburg and obtained her degree in 1988. Since then she has been a research assistant at the Faculty of Informatics at the University of Hamburg. Her research interests are computer security and privacy. She obtained her doctoral degree (PhD) in July 1992.

Karamjit S Gill, Tania Funston, Jim Thorpe, Masao Hijitaka, John Gøtze, SEAKE CENTRE, Dept of Library & Information Studies, University of Brighton, Brighton, UK.
The authors are members of the SEAKE Centre, a research centre of the University of Brighton's Faculty of Information Technology. The SEAKE Centre works to provide the research culture and ethos for undertaking

successful research and course development into human-centred systems. International links are established through collaborative research programmes, visiting research scientists, and a programme of postgraduate and doctoral research in culture and technology.

Tom Mangan, The Computability Centre, POBox 94, Warwick CV34 5WS, UK.
Tom Mangan graduated in 1983 with an honours degree in electrical and electronic engineering. He started in the field of computers and disability in 1984 as a manufacturer of equipment for disabled people. He became a committee member of the British Computer Society Disabled Specialist Group in '85 and has been secretary of the Group since '87. He is presently working full-time for The Computability Centre, a leading charity in the computers and disability field, formed by IBM UK Ltd, The British Computer Society and The University of Birmingham. Tom is also a committee member of CEPIS Social Issues Task Force and IFIP WG9.2

Shirin Madon, Dept of Information Systems, LSE, University of London, London WC2A 2AE, UK
Shirin Madon completed her PhD thesis at Imperial College, London on the impact of computer-based information systems for development planning focusing on India. She is currently a lecturer in information systems at the London School of Economics.

Vincent Mosco, School of Journalism and Communication , Carleton University, Ottawa, Canada K1S 5B6.
Vincent Mosco is professor of journalism at Carleton University. His most recent books are *The Pay-per Society: Computers and Communication in the Information Age* (Toronto: Garamond) and *Democratic Communication in the Information Age*, edited with Janet Wasko (Norwood, N.J.: Ablex).

Mayuri Odedra, Department of Information Systems & Computer Science, National University of Singapore, Lower Kent Ridge Road, Singapore 0511.
After completing her PhD on the "Transfer of I.T. to Developing Countries" at the London School of Economics in 1990, Mayuri Odedra worked as a consultant with the Management Development Programme of the Commonwealth Secretariat and for IDG West Africa Ltd as an editor of their monthly magazine - PC WORLD Africa. She joined the National University of Singapore in July 1992 as a lecturer in Information Systems.

Anton Reiter, Federal Ministry of Education and the Arts, PO Box 65, A-1014 Vienna, Austria.

Born in 1954 in Lienz (Tyrol, Austria) Dr. Anton Reiter started his studies at the University of Vienna in 1974 with the aim of becoming a higher-level general school teacher (AHS) in psychology, history and science. After nine semesters he graduated (MA, PhD in 1981) and taught at AHS from 1979 until 1984. In the course of an educational programme to establish informatics at AHS in 1984, Dr. Reiter became a member of a project group at the Federal Ministry of Education and Arts and has been working there ever since. In 1989 he became head of the Department III/15 responsible for EDP/Informatic affairs. He is lector at a college for teacher training and editor of several publications.

Morton Swimmer, Odenwaldstr. 9, 2000 Hamburg 20, Germany.
Morton Swimmer was born in New York, USA, on 12 September, 1965. After moving to Germany he studied first in England and then at the University of Hamburg. At present he is working on his masters thesis. He is also director of the Hamburg-based firm S&S International (Deutschland), a firm specialising in PC security. His research interests are computer and LAN security, in particular the problem of computer viruses.

Rian Voet, Department of Political Studies, University of Auckland, Private Bag, Auckland, New Zealand.
Rian Voet is completing her PhD on "Feminism and Citizenship: feminist critiques on a social-liberal conception of citizenship 1968-1993". She taught political theory at the Department of Politics at Leiden University and is now a lecturer in Political Theory and Gender Politics in the Department of Political Studies at the University of Auckland.

Diane Whitehouse, 460 Palmerston Boulevard, Toronto, Ontario, Canada M6G 2P1
Diane Whitehouse is currently completing her doctoral research at the London Business School into the introduction of information technology into modern languages. She possesses a degree in European Studies from the University of Bath and a masters degree in Information Systems from the London School of Economics and Political Science. She has spent several years working in the fields of future studies, human rights, and social research. She has co-authored a book on microcomputer introduction in UK university education with Rudy Hirschheim and Steve Smithson (*Microcomputers and the Humanities. Survey and Recommendations.* Ellis Horwood, 1990) and co-edited a collection of IFIP WG9.2 conference papers (Berleur et.al. *The Information Society: Evolving Landscapes.* Springer Verlag and Captus University Press, 1990). She is Secretary of IFIP Working Group 9.2.

Preface

It is easy to say that we should only use computers if they are going to do us some good, but are we always able to determine whether this is the case? The mechanisms whereby computer systems are justified are, by and large, internal to the organisations that plan to use them. However, we know that the social effect of computer use has been on such a scale that many people now describe it as heralding a new era, often referred to as the "Information Age". In this situation we need to find a framework within which both social and technological issues can be addressed, and to establish mechanisms within such a framework whereby real social accountability of information technology (IT) can be exercised on a day-to-day basis. These discussions must be not only be at the level of organisations, but must be directly relevant to the individuals that make up society. Hence the issue is both that of the social accountability of computers and of social citizenship in the information age.

T.H. Marshall defined social citizenship (as opposed to civil or political citizenship) as including

> *"a whole range from the right to a modicum of economic welfare and security to the right to share to the full in the social heritage and to live the life of a civilised being according to the standards prevailing in the society."* (Marshall, 1963, p.72)

Marshall saw a conflict between the development of social citizenship and the reliance upon economic competition. With an almost world-wide resurgence of the market as a major deciding mechanism in human affairs, it is to be expected that social citizenship finds itself under some attack. This is not just materially, in the form of curbs on state welfare benefits and educational entitlements, but also in terms of the diminution of social citizenship as a concept that we apply in our daily life. The diffusion of information technology is not unrelated to the importance given to market forces today, and so the link between IT and social accountability is one that is important to investigate. This book represents a significant attempt to address these issues in the context of the 1990s.

In this collection many different aspects of social accountability and social citizenship associated with information technology are explored and the book follows a natural progression of issues from the conceptual to the empirical, and from the individual to the global. The principal themes which are raised by the issue of social citizenship in the information age are explored in the article by Beardon, who relates the discussion to the seminal work of T. H. Marshall. The link between the growth of information technology and the reliance upon market forces is established (building upon the analysis provided by Laufer, 1991) and Marshall's belief that citizenship is essentially national is challenged. The paper sets out a conceptual framework for understanding the relationship of information technology to the various elements of social citizenship, explaining important changes that are needed to the concepts of community, equality and social progress and to the institutions of social citizenship.

The theme of citizenship and equality is explored for different groups and in different settings in the following four papers. Criticisms have been made of the traditional notion of citizenship because it refers to what is essentially the community of men, or of male interests. The concept of full social citizenship which incorporates the interests of women is explored by Voet, who compares various approaches to its redefinition and asks whether there is a role for information technology in achieving a more equitable form of citizenship. In only one of the three models she examines is there a positive role for IT. Bradley then explores the theme of citizenship in terms of the psychosocial work environment which she describes as the interaction between the environment and the individual in the context of working life. She draws distinctions between the objective and subjective conditions of work, but has also extended the scope of her research to include objective conditions outside of work (such as those relating to home or leisure) and how these may be affected by computerisation of the work environment. This paper therefore addresses a most important question for the citizenship debate, our often dual existence in working and non-working life. The impact that this division has on the roles of the two sexes and the possibilities for change offered by information technology, and especially knowledge-based systems, is explored in the context of her extensive research in Scandinavia and the USA.

The challenges and opportunities offered to disabled people in terms of realising their potential is tackled by Mangan who illustrates many of the added disadvantages that disabled people face because of the attitudes of able-bodied people. The paper describes some of the technological aids available to disabled people and makes the recommendation that, though technology has a part to play, there is still much that can be achieved through the educational system. Reiter tackles the more general responsibilities of the educational system to enable citizenship to continue to function in a world of electronic databases and electronic communication. He provides a survey of many of the important issues behind a general educational programme in informatics. The social goal of such a programme is spelled out quite clearly, "it is important that everyone should be able to become a well informed citizen in all attainable fields at all times", and this is translated into providing the necessary skills of learning "to use, select, classify, interpret and also search for information" and the need "to adopt a critical and discerning attitude towards all kinds of mass information and communication". Reiter provides details of the way that this programme has been implemented in Austria in all types of schools and summarises some of the research into its impact.

The next three papers explore social responsibility and accountability from the point of view of IT practitioners. A group of authors from the SEAKE Centre present a different type of approach to computer systems design, referred to as the "Human-Centred Systems" approach, which attempts to place human values at the centre of the design process. Inevitably, this involves questions of cultural diversity and particularly different industrial cultures. Fischer-Hübner & Swimmer consider the growing phenomenon of computer viruses and, after providing an detailed analysis of the different types of phenomena and the problems they cause, go on to discuss some possible social causes of this type of activity and ways in which it might be curtailed. They suggest that a legislative approach is fraught with difficulties of definition for there is little in the activities of a computer virus that differentiate it from any other computer program. A more promising approach, they argue, is through the development of a code of ethics for computer professionals which can refer to the general intentions of developers of software and is therefore closer to the true nature of the problem.

Concluding this section, Berleur considers how society might be forewarned about impending technologies, how it might assess them and how it might control them. Technology assessment has been defined as,

> *"the set of procedures and specific means that a society gives to itself in order to understand the issues at stake and the very nature of the development and of the present and potential use of a given technology and in order to assess its economic, social and political consequences in the short and long term."* (Petrella,1990)

Berleur presents a synopsis of the history of technology assessment, its institutions and its methods, illustrating several current opportunities for the identification of technical and social problems as they surround information technology in areas such as ISDN, Medical cards and Videotext.

The last three chapters deal with the global issues of social citizenship in an information age, with particular reference to the relationship of developing countries to advanced industrialised countries. This theme is explored in depth by Avgerou & Madon who provide a comprehensive analysis of the field and highlight the need, not simply for development through the extended use of IT, but also for the self-determination of developing countries. In the recent past "the process of development was conceived of primarily in terms of the structure and growth of the national economy and the degree of development was most often measured in terms of national income". They show how this view has been challenged and alternative analyses presented based upon concepts such as "basic needs", "dependency" and the role that such countries play in the global economic order.

Odedra takes up this theme and focuses upon the issues that have arisen in African nations as a result of the introduction of information technology. Her study shows how IT can appear as "foreign" if there is not a genuine attempt to introduce it to solve problems identified by the developing country itself and there is a genuine transfer of skills so that nationals of the country are in full control. Finally, Mosco contrasts the "The New World Order" promoted by the USA and its allies to the previous "New World Information and Communication Order" promoted through the UN by the countries of the developing world (MacBride, 1984). The media and military initiatives instigated by the developed world in recent years are examined and the impacts these have for the poor of both developed and developing countries are described. The questions raised by both these papers highlight the need to escape the national boundaries of citizenship assumed by Marshall and to strengthen the notion of global citizenship.

The idea of this book was formulated during discussions held at the first IFIP WG 9.2 Summer School held in Brighton in 1991[1]. It is appropriate that the concluding paper by Whitehouse describes the event itself. One of the aims of the organisers was that the event should itself be an exercise in citizenship and that all who participated should learn not just through the content of the week, but through the process of living and working together. The event was special, not least because of the important position given to the concept of equal representation, but also because the mix of participants and the variety of formats that led to a genuinely cooperative approach to the issues being discussed.

Together, these papers form a timely analysis of the problem of ensuring that our information systems are accountable to society. What emerges are some theoretical insights, some useful case material, some insightful analyses of particular fields and, inevitably, a realisation of the complexity of the issues involved. A particular strength of all the writers in this collection is that, whilst knowledgeable about technology and its uses, they are neither fanatically pro- or anti- information technology. They are all able to combine a discussion of the social and ethical issues with a realistic assessment of the technology, and all seek an appropriate and genuine role for the technology is the pursuit of the highest of social goals.

IFIP is the International Federation for Information Processing. It has a number of Technical Committees (TCs), one of which is concerned with "Computers & Society" (TC9). Each TC, in turn, has a number of working groups and Working Group 9.2 is concerned with "Social Accountability and Computers".

References

Laufer, R. (1991) The history of computers: an epistemological point of view. In: J. Berleur, A. Clement, R. Sizer & D. Whitehouse (eds). *The Information Society: Evolving Landscapes. Report from Namur.* Springer Verlag, New York - Captus University Publications, Toronto.

MacBride, S. (1984) *Many Voices, One World, Report by the International Commission for the Study of Communication Problems.* Unesco, New York.

Marshall, T. H. (1963) *Sociology at the Crossroads.* Heinemann, London.

Petrella, R. (1990) Les enjeux du Technology Assessment. *Journal de Réflexion sur l'Informatique,* Namur, n°18, December 1990.

1

Colin Beardon

Social citizenship in the information age

1.1 Social citizenship

In his essay on *Citizenship and Social Class*, T. H. Marshall describes citizenship as

> *a kind of basic human equality associated with the concept of full membership of a community* (Marshall, 1963, p.72)

There is a sense in which, by including the term "community" in the definition, all citizenship is going to be social, but Marshall clearly distinguishes three elements of citizenship, which he calls the civil, the political and the social. It is in the specific sense of the third of these types that we use the term "social citizenship".

The three elements of citizenship described by Marshall are as follows.

Civil citizenship is composed of:

> *the rights necessary for individual freedom - liberty of the person, freedom of speech, thought and faith, the right to own property and to conclude valid contracts, and the right to justice.*

Political citizenship involves:

> *the right to participate in the exercise of political authority or as the elector of the members of such a body.*

Social citizenship includes:

> *a whole range from the right to a modicum of economic welfare and security to the right to share to the full in the social heritage and to live the life of a civilised being according to the standards prevailing in the society.* (Marshall, 1963, p.74)

Marshall argues that these three forms of citizenship were practically indistinguishable in Britain prior to the eighteenth century, but they became fragmented around that time with each having a separate subsequent history. Civil citizenship was the first of the three forms to appear separately and this took place mainly during the eighteenth century (in Britain the culmination of this process was the Reform Act of 1832). It mainly involves rights to individual freedom within the application of universal law, and thus its primary institution is the legal system. It is expressed in the slogan, "We are all equal before the law".

Political citizenship is concerned with equal rights in the government of a community, and its main institution is the system of government. The main drive towards political citizenship took place in the nineteenth century, through campaigns to extend the franchise and to remove barriers to the exercise of political rights. In Britain, this process led to the establishment of the current parliamentary system which was essentially in place by 1918.

Social citizenship is concerned with equal distribution of (or access to) the social benefits of community, and its typical institutions are the health, education and social security services. The establishment of social citizenship has been largely a twentieth-century phenomenon, stretching in Britain from the introduction of universal free education at the end of the nineteenth century to the establishment of the welfare state in the late 1940s.

Marshall divided citizenship into these three elements to demonstrate that they are not all subject to the same analysis. Social citizenship is unlike civil or political citizenship, and not only because it was established much later. Whilst the extension of political rights was quite compatible with the existence of civil rights, as late as the early twentieth century social rights were only grudgingly acknowledged and were often considered to be in opposition to civil and political rights. The workhouse, for example, provided a minimal social security system on condition that the inmates abandoned their claim to be normal citizens. The choice for the individual was between civil and political citizenship on the one hand, and social security on the other.

Later in the twentieth century the choices facing citizens are not quite so stark (though it could be argued that the effect of the "Poll Tax" in Britain has been very similar). However, Marshall's main thesis was to point to the continuing tension between the development of social citizenship and the demands of a society based around free-market competition. Whilst civil and political citizenship can reside unproblematically within the free-market (and may even be essential elements of it), with social citizenship there is always likely to be tension.

Since Marshall made these observations, nearly forty years ago, we have seen significant ideological battles over the role of the state in social matters. Two more recent examples of the tensions to which Marshall referred are the increased importance some wish to place on individual responsibility for education, welfare and security, and the objective of reducing personal taxation at the direct expense of socialised benefits. Though these examples are derived from the British political scene this is not a purely British phenomenon for countries such as Sweden and New Zealand which were pioneers of the welfare state are also questioning whether the state can "afford" to take responsibility for traditional social rights. Certainly within

Britain, but also generally throughout the industrialised world, the forward march of social progress has become problematic. The tension has been expressed in British politics as the difference between those concerned with distributing wealth and those concerned with producing it. It is not that there is opposition in principle to the objective of social progress, but there are questions concerning the compatibility of universal, state provision of social rights and free-market principles. Central to these is the role of the state in underwriting social rights as compared to the role of individuals in making provision for their own welfare and that of their family. References to the "nanny state", for example, clearly support a major realignment in favour of free-market economics.

The continuing relevance of Marshall's observations should not hide the fact that the world is a very different place in the 1990s from what it was in the 1950s. One of the significant changes, and the one that concerns us here, has been the rapid and large-scale introduction of information and communication technology throughout the industrialised world and to some extent throughout the developing world as well. There is a need to reassess Marshall's analysis in the context of such fundamental changes in our society. If the threefold distinction between the civil, the political and the social elements of citizenship is still appropriate in an age of information, then has the historical process of their introduction been completed, stalled or placed into reverse? Is there a fourth type of citizenship that will emerge in the twenty-first century? Or does the whole analysis collapse as we stagger towards some postmodernist future that recognises only an absence of "universality" upon which, as we have shown, our existing concept of citizenship is based?

1.2 The crisis of citizenship and the crisis of legitimacy

Followers of modern cultural theory should not be surprised that in the area of social citizenship we are facing some kind of crisis, for we are frequently told that there is crisis all around us. Baudrillard, for example, would have us believe that we now live in a world of simulations in which information can only be exchanged and never used to refer to the "real" (Baudrillard, 1983), while Lyotard tells us that we must abandon the search for the meta-narrative that explains everything in a single unified scheme (Lyotard, 1984).

One of the few writers to address specifically the role of the computer in the context of contemporary crisis is Laufer, who presents an analysis that is based around the concept of legitimacy, and in particular upon the developments in legitimacy since 1790 (Laufer, 1990; 1991). Two aspects of this analysis are pertinent to our current discussion. They are those referring firstly to action, responsibility and fault, and secondly to the relationship of the public and private sectors.

Laufer holds that within the dominant rational-legal system of legitimacy established throughout Western Europe around the end of the eighteenth century, there have been three major stages. The first (from about 1790 until 1890) was based very much around the individual. In science, Newton and Kant both held that each individual has the power to know everything by direct observation of nature. In political economy it was held that a market of free and initially equal individuals, each pursuing their own economic goal, would result in the maximisation of the social goal. This concentration upon the role of the individual can also be found in the attitude to action. Responsibility was attached to individuals, as the agents of action. If I am a carpenter then I am responsible for the resulting cabinet whether or not any defect was (in our sense) my fault. This view of responsibility explains the attention paid at this time to signatures, handshakes, and a person's word, name and reputation. In this period there was simply no role for the public sector as it would have been seen as interference in the free market, and no role for social citizenship which would have been seen as undermining the system of responsibility. The community, during this period, was a community of individual entrepreneurs each with theoretically equal ability to succeed, but each facing the possibility of failure and ruin.

The second stage (from 1890 until around 1950) was based around organisations. In science it was no longer held that all knowledge could be acquired by an individual, rather that knowledge was primarily created by groups who worked within a common framework. Hence science fragmented into disciplines, each with its own methods and ways of measuring, and each with its own institutions. In political economy the problem of capital accumulation had to be faced, for this gave some entrepreneurs more power in the market than others and thus disturbed the operation of the market. The response was to allow state intervention, but only to the extent that the state could guarantee the existence of a genuine "free-market". Anti-monopoly legislation was enacted to control the size of organisations and the public sector became an economic actor, not to become a part of the market but to ensure that it returned to being "free". When it came to action, the legitimacy of an action now resided in the outcome of the action, which was measurable within one or more of the scientific disciplines. Hence an action was good in proportion to its outcome being good, which is the principle espoused by the Utilitarians (Mill, 1962). The question of how we know whether an outcome is good is not strictly a matter of science but rather one of belief in God or Progress. The community, during this period, is composed of individuals within organisations and is endowed with a sense of purpose. There is still no sense of social rights based around the individual, but only the subordination of the individual to the achievement of some higher goal, through organisation.

The third stage (since about 1945) has resulted in crisis, in which attention has focussed on method. Positivist science has been seriously undermined so that it is no longer possible for science to predict reliably the outcome of actions. The response of science has been to develop a new science of systems, which are validated by appeals to public opinion rather than to God/Progress. In political economy there has been a crisis also, resulting in a form of pragmatism. The legitimacy of action no longer resides in the outcome of an action, because science is no longer able to predict what it will be, it now resides in the method (hence the defence against bad practice is that one followed accepted procedures). The computer has occupied a central role in this developing crisis as it is the technology of pure method.

In many respects this analysis complements the observations of Marshall concerning citizenship. Marshall observed a period of developing civil rights during roughly the same period that Laufer observes the dominant idea of a natural free market (around 1800). In order that commerce can take place within a market of free entrepreneurs there must be certain basic rules: agreements must be honoured, no-one must be able to act in a way that another cannot, etc. The moral philosophy of Kant derives such rules specifically from the principle of universality (Acton, 1970). Civil rights were the natural expression of the ground rules for a market of free individuals, as Marshall makes clear,

> *civil rights [are] indispensable to a competitive market economy.*
> (Marshall, 1963, p.90)

Marshall then observes a period of emerging political rights during roughly the same period that Laufer remarks upon increasing state intervention (1800-1890). Both writers point to the growth of organisations during this period, though Marshall concentrates more on political organisations, while Laufer stresses economic and scientific institutions. Both types of organisation require the exercise of control, which ultimately comes down to the exercise of political control through some parliament. To be legitimate, this parliament must reflect public opinion and the best way to organise this is through some electoral and representative system.

Finally, Marshall observes a period in which the attempt to establish social rights comes into conflict with the free-market system. We can understand this conflict within Laufer's analysis as being the result of a confusion between culture and nature. From a cultural perspective society demands greater cooperation, equality and security, whilst from a scientific perspective society demands greater competition, inequality and risk. (From the scientific perspective of economics, wealth is maximised by the operation of a competitive market in which there must be the risk of failure; from the cultural perspective of humanism, the social objective is security through cooperation.) The epitome of this confusion between culture and nature, which Laufer sees as fundamental to the period since 1945, is the computer: a device which obeys both cultural and scientific laws.

The relationship of information technology to the problems of social citizenship are therefore far more complex than we may at first suspect. Not only does the presence of information technology provide a new environment in which the practice of social citizenship needs reappraisal, but the existence of the computer indicates a philosophical realignment in which the concept of social citizenship also needs examination. It would be meaningless to look for causes (i.e. which came first) and we should conclude that these are different aspects of the same crisis.

1.3 The information age

Ardigo (1989) describes the potential of information technology for advancing the cause of social citizenship in terms of three general areas.

(1) To ensure a fair social distribution of the social benefits of technological progress.

(2) To improve the efficiency and effectiveness of public administration and the liberal professions.

(3) To enable the best possible exercise of citizens' rights to information and their participation in decision-making.

Whilst these may be the objectives we set ourselves as social citizens, Marshall has warned us that the achievement of these aims may not be easy as they are in tension with the free-market principles that are dominant in society and may therefore be reflected in information technology.

In addressing these questions we must examine the relationship between information technology and the free-market. Bell used the term "post-industrial society" to describe the results of a shift in employment away from the traditional primary and secondary sectors (agriculture, mining, etc. and manufacturing), into the tertiary sector (information and personal services) (Bell, 1973). Whilst there undoubtedly has been such a change in industrialised countries, Bell's conclusions are controversial (see Avgerou & Madon, this volume). Nevertheless, the concept of the tertiary sector is important, for by grouping together both information services and those services central to the delivery of social citizenship, Bell highlights their very close relationship.

If information is conceived as part of the economy, then this is a way of saying that it has acquired a new type of value. Fifty years ago people did not often use the term "information", but rather spoke about "wisdom" or "knowledge". The value of wisdom and knowledge lay in the practical benefits they gave us in dealing with the world through being able to understand, predict, plan and reassess. The concept of "information" involves taking these social and contextual skills and reifying them into commodities. As commodities they possess not only a use-value, as described above, but also an exchange-value (Mosco, 1989). There is now a market in information, hence we are introduced to the concept of "value-added" information services which are defined without regard to the use-value of the information involved. The market now decides the worth of information, rather than human practices. For example, the market invests "owners" of information with considerable power if they can restrict access (e.g. through patents or copyrighting).

By placing information and personal services together in the tertiary sector of the economy, we reiterate the point that the crisis in social citizenship and the large-scale introduction of computer and communication technology are two aspects of the same process. Both in personal services and in information services we face conflict between tradition, motivated by use-value, and science, motivated by exchange-value. For citizens, the objective of a health service remains a healthy population, and the objective of information is to tell the truth, but the efficient organisation of these services at a community level seems to require the objective of lowering the cost of provision, or even showing a profit. The relationship between citizenship and an information sector of the economy is therefore highly problematic. On the one hand, responsible citizenship requires the availability of knowledge (i.e. high use-value information), whereas on the other the market is creating whatever information is profitable and pragmatically effective (i.e. high exchange-value information).

Based on this analysis, we can identify four major areas of concern. The definition of citizenship provided by Marshall centred around the key concepts of "community" and "equality" and we are interested in whether there has been any significant change in these concepts in an information age. We also know that social citizenship is very much tied to its institutions and so we are interested in the effect upon these institutions of increased use of information technology. Finally, we must address Marshall's sense of historical progression and ask whether it is possible to make social progress in an information age.

1.4 Community in the information age

A central problem posed by Marshall's concept of citizenship is that it does not explicitly say what we are citizens of. For many people, they may feel competing allegiances to their local community, social or political organisations, ethnic grouping, religion, nation, region, all humankind, all living things, or everything. Marshall was insistent that citizenship exists only at the level of the national community.

> *the citizenship whose history I wish to trace is, by definition, national* (Marshall, 1963, p.75)

There is, however, no real argument why this should be so. Clearly the nation state has been predominant in demanding allegiance and creating and moulding the institutions of citizenship, but its position by no means excludes others.

We have heard much, for example, about the role of information and communication technologies in shrinking the world and bringing us all very much closer together. Whilst it would be factually wrong to hold that all, or anything like the majority, of the population of the earth is in daily contact by electronic means, there exist trends which undermine national autonomy. The globalisation of production and exchange means that many people are in ambiguous situations, being born into the culture of one nation, yet operating within the industrial culture of another, whilst possibly living in yet a third. Furthermore, the creation of supranational political bodies, such as the European Community, pose further challenges to the primacy of national citizenship.

The most important loosening of our association of citizenship with the nation state is caused by the problems of developing countries. Whilst the concept of national citizenship is compatible with civil and political citizenship and provides the basis for the exploitation of colonies, it comes into conflict with social citizenship over the question of the equality of social rights between coloniser and colonised. Here again one sees the tension between a concept of (universal) citizenship and the operations of the free market. Richer donor nations give aid to developing countries for reasons that are largely self-centred. They either address specific short-term problems faced by the donor nation (to use up surplus production, to create future markets, etc.), or they address the donor nation's own strategic problems (such as the maintenance of developing countries at a minimal level to fulfill some allotted role). Either way, there is little altruism in this kind of governmental aid. Aid born of citizenship (or "humanitarian aid" as the politicians have come to describe it) is of a different kind, attempting to address the problems that are perceived by developing countries themselves, and perhaps helping them develop in a way that redefines their relationship with the industrialised countries. What is clear is that a large proportion of information technology provided under various schemes to developing countries does not advance the interests of the recipients (Odedra, this volume). What is less evident is the role that information technology might play in the self-determination of nations and whether such a role might require different forms of technology.

The problems of developing countries are one area where the application of social citizenship has become problematic as a result of a new international perspective which is partly created by information and communication technology. There are other examples that could be explored, not least the role of information technology in developing a sense of allegiance to the planet as a response to the environmental crisis. Gorz, for example, argues that technology has provided us with the means to achieve basic social rights but that the drive for more and more advanced material benefits threatens to be environmentally dangerous (Gorz, 1982). Marshall's definition of social citizenship refers to the prevailing standards in a community, but many would argue that these standards themselves come under scrutiny in an age of advancing technology. Gorz's comments are relevant to our debate because he sees a specific role for information technology in providing the means to maintain social rights whilst restraining the need for material growth.

There are many more examples of the way that the concept of national citizenship has come under question in recent history, some more and some less clearly related to information technology. It is fair to say that, for a variety of reasons, many people today feel a sense of multiple allegiance and perceive a sense of social citizenship to communities beyond simply that of their own nation. The issue of equality between communities, as well as that of equality within a community, is therefore quite clearly on the agenda (Mosco, this volume).

1.5 Equality in the information age

The concept of "equality" requires reassessment in an age of information technology from two standpoints. We must be sure that we retain equality in the light of material and legal changes in society related to the introduction of information technology, and we must re-examine the very concept of equality in the light of cultural changes that accompany the large-scale introduction of the technology.

We need first to examine the principle of equality before the law. It has long been observed that each of us now possesses an abstract form: a set of data records distributed over computer systems that record our daily transactions. Increasingly, decisions are being taken about citizens on the basis of their "data shadow" even though it is not known whether it is completely accurate. The principle of civil citizenship, that of equality before the law, may need to be revised to include the right for real citizens to be the subjects of equality and not some reconstruction of them as data. Perhaps there is a need for a fourth element of citizenship during the information age, and which we might expect to see advanced through the twenty-first century. It might be called "information citizenship" and include the right of citizens to be sure that all decisions that affect them are only taken on the basis of information that is accurate, relevant and available for inspection.

The second issue of equality is that of equality of power. Put simply: if information is power, then the unequal distribution of information processing capability creates an unequal distribution of power. Within the model of a competitive market economy, it is accepted as legitimate that the advantages of using technology accrue to the person who is prepared to invest in it. Within the social sphere, the traditions of the market economy have been copied without careful examination. Is it appropriate for computing power to be placed almost exclusively in the hands of the administrators of social policy, and not in the hands of citizens? This is not only a question of purchasing systems for the use of non-administrators: it could be something as simple as arranging the seating so that all parties can see what is being displayed on a computer screen.

As well as the need to safeguard our traditional equality, there is also a need to examine the concept of "equality". By adopting simplistic methods, information technology tends to confuse normality with equality. Economies of scale that are necessary to establish a mass market, in the name of equal opportunity, often result in the early establishment of norms which exclude specific groups. Individuals with special needs can be excluded from the social process because they do not warrant extra investment. For example, at the physical level, people with disabilities may be excluded from information because of the nature of the interface (Mangan, this volume). At a non-physical level, people who do not recognise or agree with the adopted method of conceptualisation or expression may be similarly disadvantaged. The aggregate effect may well be to force our culture into some straitjacket to which it will not easily fit, causing frictions with affected groups.

This is not to say that later, through the establishment of more "socially-aware" standards, the rights of minorities might not be safeguarded, but this is achieved only when the market is ready. A new legal requirement to address some problem of access may make technological products more expensive, but this can provide a welcome fillip to an established market. From an economic point of view, social awareness can be accommodated once the market exists and the unit cost is low enough to sustain a small increase in price.

This process may operate with respect to the physical aspects of computer systems, but we have seen that the computer is the technology of method. How, then, are we to define equality today? In the period of the individual, equality was the equality of the entrepreneur to speculate. In the period of organisations, equality was equality of access to the results of action. Today, in the period of information, equality means equal representation in the methods adopted.

However, computers are frequently criticised for adopting very formal, analytical approaches to problem-solving. These may be shown to be effective in certain restricted areas but are not universally valid. Significant sections of the population do not accept the legitimacy of computer-based reasoning, especially in areas concerned with caring for the needs of individuals. This has been expressed in various ways: for example, we hear that women do not always agree with the "male logic" of computers, or that inhabitants of the developing world do not always accept the "logic" of the developed world (Voet, this volume; Odedra, this volume). There is a need to develop mechanisms whereby equality can find expression within our preoccupation with method, and such mechanisms will reside within the institutions of citizenship.

1.6 The institutions of citizenship in the information age

Computer technology is now heavily used in the institutions of citizenship (the legal system, the parliamentary system, the social welfare, health and education systems) and this raises the question, are the computerised institutions of citizenship subject to social control? It is now a widely held belief that some systems are so large and complex that they have assumed a life of their own. No one person has an overview of them or can reliably predict how they may behave. In the event of a failure we will be quite unable to say who was responsible or who was at fault and we will probably conclude that it was either an "operator error" or a "systems error".

If it is argued that operators are the cause of such failures, it is because of a belief that human beings are the weakest link in semi-automated systems. The conclusion is then drawn that systems can only be made more reliable by the replacement of any remaining human functions by machines. This is a good example of the battle between nature and culture that is endemic to our age. Science has presented us with the technology of method, but when applying it we wish to know who is responsible. As nobody can be responsible for methods we find no satisfactory answer. The necessity to find some answer means that we act pragmatically and go for the nearest thing to an agent, which is the operator (Perrow, 1984). Given the conceptual structure we have adopted it would be more honest to claim that no-one is responsible (in the traditional sense) and that the breakdown was indeed a "systems error". The discussion should not end here, however, for the question is then raised, what is the nature of responsibility for systems?

If responsibility cannot lie with operators and it is impossible to determine precise causes and effects within systems, then responsibility can only lie in one of two places. Either the owners of systems are responsible or their designers are. We saw the emergence of the idea that owners are responsible in the court case following the sinking of the ferry ship "The Herald of Free Enterprise", when an attempt was made to introduce the legal concept of "corporate manslaughter". The role of the designer in the market economy is as an entrepreneur like any other. The "scientific" designer attempts to squeeze responsibility out of the process altogether. The "user" of a system is seen only as a provider of data for the design process, and the resulting system is derived according to "objectively true" procedures. There have been some notable exceptions to this in design practices which seek to provide a traditional, cultural context for design (Kyng, 1991; Funston *et al.*, this volume).

Little attention has also been paid to whether different design behaviours should be adopted in the public and the private sectors. If any difference has been observed between the two practices, it is that public services are believed to be inefficient or bureaucratic. It is then argued that this should be remedied by introducing into public sector institutions the same information-processing methods used in the private sector. This objective has been followed in Britain by attempting to contract out public sector administration to the lowest bidder. Though existing public sector employees are allowed to bid, it does not matter who wins the contract since the terms of competition with the private sector have been established.

But it is by no means obvious that the objectives of systems in the two different contexts are the same. To take but one example, who is the "user" of a computer system in the public sector? Is it the same person, or group of people, who are the "user" in the private sector? This is not a rhetorical question, for if the citizen is the true user of public sector computing facilities, whereas the entrepreneur is the user in the private sector, then the privatisation of public services in the name of efficiency is undermining progress towards social citizenship.

1.7 Social progress in the information age

A noticeable feature of change over the past twenty or so years has been the decline in the use of the term "progress". The goal of seeking to improve the lot of some or all citizens underlies Ardigo's three areas, cited above (pp.5-6), but they can seem almost anachronistic. The postmodern world does not think like this, it tries only to maintain and to avoid, never to achieve.

Information technology is a part of this realignment. The ready availability of powerful technology has led to our having access to far more information than we know what to do with, with the result that we treat symptoms rather than causes. We see the computer as arriving "just in time" to solve some administrative problem, but really it arrives "just in time" to prop up a system that would otherwise have become untenable (Weizenbaum, 1976). Had the computer not been available, a radical rethink of the problem would have been required and a new approach adopted. In part the problem lay in the enormous investment that there is in procedures that involve computerised systems. The cost of adopting new procedures outweighs their advantage in any particular case, and so the computerised system becomes inherently conservative. The technology of pure method is the technology for a community which has lost its sense of direction.

In its decline, the concept of "progress" has been replaced by the concept of "sustainability" (just as the positivism of science gave way to the science of systems). Sustainability is not the distinguishing feature of any particular theory or movement, but rather the fundamental paradigm as we move into the twenty-first century. Sustainability means that we do not act to improve situations, but rather act to maintain balance. We overcome problems rather than engineer new situations. Hence our political systems are presented as gigantic balancing acts, pursued in order to return us to some imaginary state of stability when life can begin again. We are constantly "in a mess", and we are looking for leaders who will "get us out of it". The science of systems and the concept of sustainability provide the context within which the fight for social citizenship will have to be fought.

1.8 Conclusion

It has been argued that a close relationship exists between the problems of advancing social citizenship and the nature of society in an information age. This relationship is complex, involving both the application of the principles of social citizenship in a society dominated by information and communication technology, and a reappraisal of the concept of social citizenship itself. It touches on many issues: the role of information technology in the relationship of developed to developing countries, equality of opportunity with respect to information technology, the rights of citizens with respect to information, the extent to which computerised systems involve social risks, the involvement of users in the design of systems, and many more. In addition, we must be aware that the very language of social citizenship is in tension with the language of the information age; that humanitarian goals are supposed to be subordinate to economic priorities. This paper cannot resolve this conflict, however its aim has been to clarify the dichotomy and elucidate the relevance of the issues surrounding the development of information processing systems in relation to the goal of enhanced social citizenship.

References

Acton, H. B. (1970) *Kant's Moral Philosophy.* Macmillan, London.

Ardigo, A. (1989) *New Technology and Social Citizenship.* Paper presented to the International Workshop on Human Centred Systems Design, Brighton Polytechnic 22-24 September 1989.

Baudrillard, J. (1983) *Simulations.* Semiotext(e), New York.

Bell, D. (1973) *The coming of the post-industrial society.* Heinemann, London.

Gorz, A. (1982) *Farewell to the Working Class.* Pluto Press, London.

Kyng, M. (1991) Designing for cooperation: cooperating in design. *Communications of the ACM,* **34**, 12, pp.64-73.

Laufer, R. (1990) The history of computers: an epistemological point of view. In: J. Berleur, A. Clement, R. Sizer & D. Whitehouse (eds). *The Information Society: Evolving Landscapes. Report from Namur.* Springer Verlag, New York - Captus University Publications, Toronto.

Laufer, R. (1991) The social acceptability of A I systems: legitimacy, epistemology and marketing. Proceeding of IFIP-GI Conference on

Opportunities and Risks of Artificial Intelligence Systems (ORAIS '89). Hamburg, July 1989.

Lyotard, J-L. (1984) *The Postmodern condition.* Manchester University Press, Manchester.

Marshall, T. H. (1963) *Sociology at the Crossroads.* Heinemann, London.

Mill, J. S. (1962) *Utilitarianism.* Collins, London.

Mosco, V. (1989) *The pay-per society: computers and communication in the information age.* Garramond Press, Toronto.

Perrow, C. (1984) *Normal accidents: living with high-risk technologies.* Basic Books, New York.

Weizenbaum, J. (1976) *Computer power and human reason.* W H Freeman, San Francisco.

2

Rian Voet

Women as citizens and the role of information technology

It has already become a cliché to say that even in our modern western liberal democracies women are second-class citizens. Very rarely, however, the normative question has been asked, "what would feminist citizenship look like?" This question lays at the centre of this paper. Within the context of the summer school "Social Citizenship in the Information Age" a second question will be addressed, namely the question, "how information technology can help us to advance such a feminist citizenship".

This paper presents an alternative to the two main answers to this question: what a feminist citizenship would look like, that have been proposed in feminist literature on citizenship. Instead of offering women exactly the same citizenship that men have and instead of reinterpreting citizenship through a female perspective, this paper will argue for a new route, namely that of reinterpreting citizenship from a feminist perspective. Although information technology is extremely useful in the first option in which women are offered exactly the same citizenship as men have, it is hardly useful at all in the other two options.

2.1 The present situation: women as second-sex citizens

What is the current situation of women as citizens and does it make a difference whether we answer this question with regard to women's rights or with regard to women's participation?

With respect to the sorts of *participation* that we usually associate with citizenship, women's situation is indeed very bad. Women's participation in decision-making bodies and in the official labour-market is relatively low. Women are hardly active within the army. They have much less property than men and are therefore less powerful as consumers and producers.

With respect to the *rights* which the influential British sociologist T. H. Marshall associated with citizenship, women's situation is not much better. In his article, *Citizenship and Social Class*, Marshall distinguishes three kinds of citizenship rights: civil, political and social (Marshall, 1965). Civil citizenship is that part which is necessary for individual freedom: "liberty of the person, freedom of speech, thought, faith, the right to own property and to conclude valid contracts and the right to justice". Political citizenship is "the right to participate in the exercise of political power, as a member of a body invested with political authority or as an elector of the members of such a body". Social citizenship is "the right to a modicum of economic welfare security regardless of the position on the labour market and the right to share to the full of the social heritage and to live the life of a civilised being according to the living standard prevailing in society" (Marshall, 1965, p78). Marshall's main thought is that our society tends to give all citizens these rights; our society will eventually give all mature, rational citizens full citizenship rights.

Feminists have accused Marshall of historical inaccuracy. While Mary MacIntosh accuses Marshall of ignoring the fact that women received all these three citizenship rights much later than men did, Margaret Stacey and Marion Price say that Marshall fails to note that the "historical order of the emancipation of women is different from that which was followed in the case of men. ... Women were in the end accorded politic citizenship before they were granted full civil citizenship." (MacIntosh, 1984; Stacey and Price, 1981, p. 48.)

Besides, these so-called universal citizenship rights have not been fully realised for women, according to many feminists. Women have eventually received suffrage and their *political* rights are now equal to men's. Nevertheless, when political groups are defending men's interests, they are perceived as representing citizens' interests. When, on the contrary, political groups are defending women's interests, they are perceived as representing specific group interests. Speaking further about *civil* citizenship rights, it must be noticed that although approximately all civil rights are formally equal for both sexes, they are usually not guaranteed within the private sphere of the family. This fact has more negative consequences for women than for men, because women need rights more than men do within private heterosexual-relationships. Women within these relationships have generally less power than their male partners and spend more time in the private sphere. *Social* citizenship rights, such as the right to unemployment benefits, pensions and social security, often require of citizens a curriculum vitae full of paid jobs in order to receive these rights. Many housewives are consequently denied an independent entitlement to these social rights.

There is no need to elaborate on these themes. So much has already been written about the empirical situation of women as citizens. Ruth Lister, Ann Phillips and Caroline Ellis describe women's citizenship situation in Britain (Lister, 1990; Phillips 1991; Ellis, 1991). Helga Maria Hernes and Birthe Siim do the same for Scandinavia (Hernes, 1988, Siim, 1988). Bettina Cass focuses on Australia and Trudie Knijn analyses the Netherlands (Cass, 1990;

Knijn, 1991). Arnold Whittick, finally, describes the history of the international women citizenship organisation and the results of its struggles (Whittick, 1979).

It is now more important to ask what the alternative for women's current citizenship would look like.

2.2 The first option: exactly the same citizenship as men

Although feminists in the past were very negative about Marshall, recently they have changed their attitude. Feminists no longer perceive Marshall's account on citizenship as descriptive but rather as normative. What Marshall actually intended to say, according to these latter feminists was that citizenship *should* be universal (Siim, 1988; Lister, 1990; Vogel, 1989).

This leads us to the first feminist answer to the question "what would feminist citizenship look like', namely that because citizenship should be universal: women should have exactly the same citizenship as men have. Feminists have suggested three versions of this answer (Okin, 1989; Dietz, 1987; Siim, 1988; Hernes, 1988).

A first version of equal citizenship is that citizenship rights which already exist for men should be *formally* extended to women. Welfare rights should not have any reference to gender. This would, however, not immediately provide the same social citizenship rights for men and women. The law may for instance indicate that a person who provides unpaid care for someone else will have no right to social citizenship rights. Some feminists have therefore argued for a second meaning of equal citizenship.

A second version is that the state should make sure that *everyone will have the same citizenship rights*. As our rights are inherently connected to our positions, either each position should have the same consequences for citizenship rights or all of us should have the same positions. Thus, either housewives should receive equal social citizenship rights or housework should be equally divided amongst all adults. The European Community guidelines that forbid direct *and* indirect discrimination between the sexes in labour, social security and pensions, work upon the principle that each position should have the same consequences for citizenship rights. Yet, most national states still have to develop law that implements these guidelines. Feminist organisations can play an important role in defining exactly what kind of law should be developed and how it should be implemented.

There is, furthermore, a third, and even more radical egalitarian version of equal citizenship, which is that every one should make the *same use of citizenship rights*. Within this perspective too, arguments have been made for an equal division for paid and unpaid work, but other arguments have been added. In order to reach the same use of rights, other kinds of sources should also be equally distributed between the sexes. More capital, cultural capital, time, space, mobility, safety and information should therefore be given to women (Lister, 1990; Hernes, 1988; Siim, 1988). Furthermore, it would be necessary that both sexes have the same kinds of capabilities and skills. When this is not the case, women should receive special education, training in public speech, practice in public decision-making processes. If even this is insufficient to achieve the same level of citizenship rights, women may be obliged to provide the same amount of participation in politics, the official economy and the army. It will be obvious that this meaning of citizenship goes into more much detail about the conditions for and substance of participation.

These three versions of equal citizenship gradually move in the direction of a controlled society. In order to bring the ideal of equality nearer, more and more severe measures are being proposed. Not being satisfied with formal equal rights, feminists have also demanded equality in the conditions of citizenship and equality in citizenship participation. Determined feminists have excused the use of all "necessary means" by the Great Ideal of Equality itself.

Now, information technology is seen as crucial in this process of control on the state level, the individual level and the group level.

Information technology may provide a *state* with information about people's actual situations, so that the government will recognise where inequalities appear and must be balanced. If, for example, it is observed that a large number of children are living in a particular neighbourhood, the government may provide that neighbourhood with more parks and child-care facilities.

Information technology is also for *individuals* a valuable source. It not only provides useful *work* when it gives individuals information about their society and the possibilities for development, but it is also a useful empowering instrument to *work with*. It gives people an extra skill. For instance, information technology can bring one divorced woman into contact with another, so that they can buy a house together, thus avoiding the increasing costs of rented accommodation. Computer technology also gives opportunities for ordering shopping and for arranging child-care. It may give information about investment, speculation, education and employment. Finally, it provides individuals with the tools to have an information job at home and to set up networks with other people. This brings us to the group level.

On a *group* level, information technology is extremely useful in order to mobilise people in similar situations, with similar interests or problems. Divorced women, to continue that example, may easily communicate with each other, discuss what kind of divorce law should be advocated, mobilise other divorcees to influence parliament and to operate as an interest group in court. Information technology may also be extremely useful in mobilising home-workers in the information branch to sue their employers, demand better payment, insurance or social security.

Information technology, therefore, is not only an important source in the process of implementing equal citizenship rights for both sexes, but also a crucial tool in order to make equal use of these rights.

Nevertheless, the potential usefulness of information technology within this option does not relieve us from the task of having to evaluate the option itself. According to the proposals which we considered, a more equal distribution of rights will be reached and more people will exercise citizenship as we understand it at present. It will probably lead to more careerism, to a confirmation of liberal representative democracy and to more consumerism. I do not want here to discuss the alternatives to liberal citizenship, such as republican and communitarian citizenship. Arguments for these sorts of citizenship may also be presented from other perspectives than feminist ones. What is specifically important for feminists is that an extension of men's citizenship to women does not necessarily alter the old connotations of citizenship with maleness. It will rather fit women into a male order. Of course, it is perfectly reasonable to argue that this process of incorporating women into the current idea of citizenship will eventually also change the meaning of citizenship. But why not take a more active attitude in this matter and accelerate this process?

There is a second disadvantage of the option of equal citizenship, which is that in order to abolish second-class citizenship, it may also abolish differences that are really positive for citizenship. Society will be much stronger if different groups participate in it and offer their diverse values and experiences to it. Then, a state will be more prepared to change, will be more balanced, will be less likely to be corrupt and will be more lively. Only in a pluralist society, citizens' participation will not be superfluous.

To summarise, although this notion of feminist citizenship abolishes inequality, it may also abolish differences that are really positive for citizenship.

2.3 The second option: reinterpreting citizenship from a female perspective

Several feminists point out that women should not be satisfied with an equal distribution of citizenship, but should also demand that the old connotations of citizenship and manhood should disappear. Citizenship should no longer be connected to notions of soldiering, paid work, revolution, abstract justice, the public sphere and generality, because in effect this will privilege a view of men as citizens (Benton, 1991; Fraser, 1989, 1990; Pateman, 1988).

Feminists within this second option argue therefore that women should reinterpret citizenship by taking a female perspective. Once we suppose that the citizen is female, these feminists argue, then many existing connotations of citizenship will be extremely puzzling.

Let me give two examples of feminist arguments along this line and ways in which they reinterpret citizenship from a female perspective.

Bettina Cass has argued that any discussion of gender and social citizenship must begin with a re-evaluation of the concept of (in)dependency. According to her, citizenship is now often associated with independent economic and political citizens. According to Cass, women do not enter both "economic life" and "public life" in this way, "but as people who bear in their everyday lives, their psychological, emotional and material lives, and who are correspondingly seen to bear, the responsibility to care for others" (Cass, 1990, p. 11). She argues that "currently, men's independence is predicated on their relative freedom from the responsibility for caring work, that is, independence is a masculine prerogative. At the same time, and as a direct consequence, women's dependence, both on men and the state, is constructed because they are responsible for the relationships of caring in domestic and personal life. It is not women's "dependency" therefore which is the problem for public policy, but men's "independence". ... Men cannot be accorded full citizenship if they do not fulfil their caring obligation in private life" (Cass, 1990, p. 15). By this female reinterpretation, citizenship should not be associated with independency from care, but with a responsibility in care.

Kathleen Jones undertakes a similar enterprise. This time, however, the reinterpretation takes place not from the perspective of the individual woman, but of the women's movement. According to Jones we need to "articulate the historically evolving content of the women's movement which suggests a transformed theory and practice of citizenship" (Jones, 1990, p. 783). This transformation will have several elements according to Jones. The transformed theory will focus on identity and identification. It will see the body in relation to the body politic. This new theory will reveal sexual harassment as a political strategy to hinder women's political presence. A shift from armed defence to empowerment as the model of citizenship will be noticed. It will have "the personal is political" as its motto, so that new duties, responsibilities and rights will arise. The transformed theory will, according to Jones, engender democracy in more bodies and for more human forms of organisations. It will consist of a critique of the nation-state. It will locate political action also within the private realm and it will "embrace the cherished ideals and precious human values that flow from the social world of women" (Jones, 1990, p. 795).

In short, within the second answer to the question of "what feminist citizenship would look like', rights and participation are reinterpreted from the perspectives of woman and women. Citizenship rights are no longer automatically constructed in the way in which law or customs have constructed the "right of privacy" or "the right of justice". Women may interpret Marshall's formulations of citizenship rights for their own purposes. They may argue that the right of justice should lead to a prohibition of pornography or that the right of privacy should also be guaranteed within the family. Women may also extend Marshall's list with their own list of citizenship rights. Women have already claimed body-rights, rights on child-care and maternity-leave.

When citizenship is reinterpreted from a female perspective, information technology will have a limited use. After all, many feminists have already pointed out that information technology generally accepts current definitions and concepts. If feminists want to change the world in a "female way', information technology can only be used if it will be steered by women who alter current meanings. For instance, it would be very useful if statistical information about the division of resources between households were extended to include information about the division of resources within households. Yet, there are still too few (influential) women working in the creative side of information technology to make such a change.

Apart from the practical problem of the limited use of information technology, there are also other, and more serious, problems involved in this option of reinterpreting citizenship from a female perspective.

Although the two mentioned approaches by Cass and Jones have many stimulating aspects, they have one problem in common: they presuppose that everything women do is good. If we must find the feminist alternative in the experiences of individual women or in the practices of the women's movement, then every critical distance will be impossible. No other criteria will be needed. We cannot accept this idea. Women, although "oppressed', have their share in the continuation of a sexist world. Their views are not necessarily better than men's. The oppression does not give them the honour of being the people with the vocation to know the truth about everything or even about gender-issues. Indeed, one could argue that as a result of women's oppression women's views are slightly distorted and therefore we should not take them too seriously.

Furthermore, even if we think women's views on or experiences with a specific theme are the best, it is not necessarily true that they are the best for citizenship. After all, citizenship does not include everything but merely refers to an ideal of civic rights and action that is distinct from other aspects of life. The ideal of motherhood may be perfectly reasonable within parenting but not within citizenship. As Mary Dietz argues: *"There is no reason to think that mothering necessarily induces commitment to democratic practices. Nor are there good grounds for arguing that a principle like "care for vulnerable human life" (as noble as that principle is) by definition encompasses a defence of participatory citizenship"* (Dietz, 1987, p.15).

A last disadvantage of this second option (of what feminist citizenship would look like) is that it represses differences amongst women. Although women are often in similar situations of repression, their positions are definitively not identical. Not for nothing have black and lesbian feminists accused main-stream feminism of presupposing in its theory a white, heterosexual married woman. Feminists should take this criticism seriously and incorporate differences within their theories. It is not only almost impossible to abolish differences of race and sexuality, but also undesirable. These differences, furthermore, may not only have negative effects (in respect of discrimination), but also positive effects (in respect of diversity) for politics and culture.

To conclude, the second option of citizenship is critical towards current "male" notions of citizenship and reinterprets the links between gender and citizenship. Yet, in doing this it gives far too stereotypical and uniform a picture of women as a whole and wrongly presupposes that what women think is good and will therefore be good for citizenship.

2.4 The third option: reinterpreting citizenship starting from a feminist perspective

Thus far I have indicated two different answers feminists usually give on the question of "what feminist citizenship should be". The first answer is that women should have exactly the same citizenship as men have at the moment. This answer alters the distribution of citizenship but does not remove its deep connotation with maleness. The second answer is that citizenship should be redefined from a female perspective. This answer, however, presupposes that what women do is automatically good and will be good for citizenship.

It might seem that if we cannot accept the assumptions of the second answer, then we will need to go back to the first answer (the equal distribution of citizenship) and accept the traditional connotations and meanings of citizenship. It is within this dichotomy of equality versus difference that the debate between feminists has been trapped for a long time. Either feminists had to accept the male view on life and extend it to women, or they had to put forward the female view on life as better.

Both answers are unsatisfactory and there is a third possible answer. After all, citizenship can not only be revised from a female perspective, but also from a feminist perspective. This implies that not everything that women say or do is perceived as right. This third answer implies further that abolition of exclusion is not enough, because inclusion too may be a problem. Whether it is will depend on the terms of inclusion. Let me give an example of what I mean.

Anne Phillips has shown how there is a strong connotation of citizenship with fraternity (Phillips, 1984). When the French Revolution of 1798 proclaimed the citizenship ideals of equality, liberty and fraternity on the level of the national state, Phillips argues, two things went wrong. Not only did the revolutionaries in their self-proclaimed universalism overlook their sisters, but they also made women serve the fraternity of men. From that point onwards, fraternal citizenship was a corollary: it was universal *and* only applied to men. According to Phillips it would be no alternative to argue for feminist citizenship in the form of sisterhood instead. *"Whether the ideal be sisterhood or brotherhood, the language of siblings imposes its own constraints. It identifies a common heritage, some shared experience that sets us apart from the rest of the world"* (Phillips, 1984, p. 239). It presupposes unity which restricts plurality and heterogeneity and is destructive for solidarity in the end. *"We should not act as if the only solidarity worth its name is the one that unites through every aspect of our existence. Rather, we should think of socialist (RV; here feminist) unity as a complicated - maybe even painful - construction from many different solidarities, some of which will inevitably be in conflict"* (Phillips, 1984, p. 241).

Phillips thus criticises women's exclusion from citizenship by the term "fraternity" and argues simultaneously that it would not be a good alternative to choose sisterhood. We have to be aware that some "unities" may be repressive for others and for ourselves as well. Citizenship should be combined with plurality and heterogeneity.

This provides a clear problem for feminists. They can accept neither inequality nor a uniform equality. Feminists must therefore engage in a debate about which differences are acceptable and which are not. Which differences are negative and will threaten citizenship? Which differences are, in contrast, positive and will strengthen citizenship? These questions are especially pressing because of our "post-modern" condition. Fragmentation of ideals, life-styles and identities can be noticed. The idea of one absolute truth as the perception of human being as autonomous, rational and calculating has been questioned. Increasingly reality is perceived as contingent and not proceeding logically to equality and liberty. Indeed, the substance of these values of equality and liberty may not be the same for all individuals and all groups.

Information technology is of little practical use in repositioning us and helping us to create a citizenship that is human-universal and pluralist at the same time. The only practical thing we could do is to open a mail-box on the issue of feminist citizenship. Information technology could perhaps be more useful because if provides an important analogy. Thinking about information technology could enlarge our minds on the theme of feminist citizenship. Reflections on the endless possibilities of files, sub-directions and directions could open up our minds to the endless variations of universality and plurality.

Iris Marion Young has already been helpful in distinguishing three different meanings of universal citizenship, namely "universality as the inclusion and participation of everyone in public life and in the democratic process', "universality as formulating laws and rules in general terms, which apply to all citizens in the same way" and "universality as taking a universal perspective and leaving all perceptions behind, which are the result of people's particular experiences and social positions" (Young, 1989, pp. 273-274). Young argues that, from a feminist perspective, universality as inclusion is desirable, but universality as equal treatment and generality should be rejected. She prefers a differentiated citizenship with special rights and a special political group-representation for women and other disadvantaged groups. Yet in putting forwards her alternative, she falls back in what I have called the second option "redefining citizenship from a female perspective". Although she emphasises that women do not have a special nature, she stills accepts the view that what women do is right, because women are a disadvantaged group. Women therefore appear to have more insight in the matters that concern them than others (compare also Young, 1990).

If we do not want to accept these assumptions, but still want to continue construing universal citizenship that allows for differences, Alessandro Ferrara's approach may be promising (Ferrara, 1990). Ferrara is not writing within a feminist perspective. He is involved in the project of integrating liberalism and communitarianism. He is searching for a universalism that accepts the fact that our values and identities differ radically. Ferrara finds three concepts of universality that try to do this. He rejects "empty" procedural universalism and "too full" communitarian universalism and prefers instead a combination, that is "prudential universalism". He reconstructs the ability to communicate *and* the competence to judgment or phronesis as a common transcultural basis between people. According to Ferrara, phronesis is "the competence possessed by all human beings to various degrees to assign priorities, in the absence of established priorities, to conflicting values in the service of the flourishing of an identity" (Ferrara, 1990, p. 33). In this inter-subjective way particular priorities and identities can be negotiated in order to come of some kind of ad-hoc universalism.

Feminists can make use of Ferrara's approach, combining it with their specific feminist critique and go beyond "prudential universalism". Alternatively, they may start from an analysis of plurality, distinguishing a rather harmless plurality of opinions (which I would prefer to call pluralism), from a plurality of groups, interests, identities and sorts of political representatives. While the first is very easy to combine with political equality, the latter meanings of plurality will cause many problems. One important question for the current debate is whether plurality should be constructed on the basic level of citizenship rights or only on the surplus level of participation. Affirmative action is a modern issue which is very likely to encourage a debate on the several meanings of universal and plural citizenship and on the distinction between (negative) inequality and (positive) difference.

Many people will give many different answers to the question of "what feminist citizenship should look like". I have argued here that although the third answer of redefining citizenship starting from a feminist perspective is the most complicated, it is not desirable to be satisfied with the answers of "giving women exactly the same citizenship as men have" and of "redefining citizenship from a female perspective".

References

Benton, Sarah (1991) Gender, Sexuality and Citizenship. In: G. Andrews (ed.) *Citizenship*. Lawrence & Wishart, London, pp. 151-163.

Cass, Bettina (1990) Gender and Social Citizenship: Women's pursuit of citizenship in the 1990's, with particular reference to Australia. Paper for the 24th annual conference of the Social Policy Association, University of Bath, U.K., 10-12 July 1990.

Dietz, Mary G. (1987) Context is All: Feminism and Theories of Citizenship. *Daedalus* **116**, 4, Fall 1987, pp. 1-24.

Ellis, Caroline (1991) Sisters and Citizens. In: G. Andrews (ed.) *Citizenship*. Lawrence & Wishart, London, pp. 235-243.

Ferrara, Alessondro (1990) Universalisms: procedural, contextualist and prudential. In: D. Rasmussen (ed.) *Universalism vs. Communitarianism. Contemporary debates in ethics.* The MIT Press, Cambridge, Mass., pp. 11-39.

Fraser, Nancy (1989) *Unruly Practices. Power, Discourse and Gender in Contemporary Social Theory*. Polity Press, Cambridge.

Fraser, Nancy (1990) Gender, Citizenship and the Public Sphere: Toward a Feminist Reconstruction of Habermas. In: S. Sevenhijsen (ed.), Anna Maria van Schuurman centrum 1990, Utrecht, pp. 76-121.

Hernes, Helga Maria (1988) The Welfare State Citizenship of Scandinavian Women. In: K.B. Jones and A. G. Jinasdittir (eds) *The Political Interests of Gender: developing theory and research with a feminist face*, Sage, London, pp. 187-214.

Jones, Kathleen B. (1990) Citizenship in a woman-friendly polity. *Signs: Journal of Women in Culture and Society,* **15**, 4, pp. 781-812.

Knijn, Trudie (1991) *Citizenship, Care and Gender in the Dutch Welfare State*. Paper presented to the European Feminist Research Conference

"Women in a Changing Europe", University of Aalborg, Denmark, August 18-22, 1991, pp. 1-13.

Lister, Ruth (1990) Women, Economic Dependency and Citizenship. *Journal of Social Policy*, **19**, 4, pp. 445-467.

MacIntosh, Mary (1984) The Family, Regulation and the Public Sphere. In G. McLennon, D. Held and S. Hall (eds), *State and Society in Contemporary Britain. A critical Introduction*, Polity Press, Cambridge.

Marshall, T. H. (1965) Citizenship and social class. In *Class, Citizenship and Social Development*, Anchor, New York.

Okin, Susan Miller (1989) *Justice, Gender and the Family*. Basic Books, New York.

Pateman, Carole (1988) *Women's Citizenship: Equality, Difference and Subordination*. Paper for the "Workshop on 'Equality' and 'Difference': Gender Dimensions in Political Thought, Justice and Morality", European University Institute, Florence, December 1988, pp. 1-30.

Phillips, Anne (1984) Fraternity. In B. Pimlott (ed.) *Fabian Essays in Socialist Thought*. Heinemann, London, pp. 230-241.

Phillips, Anne (1991) Citizenship and Feminist Politics. In G. Andrews (ed) *Citizenship*. Lawrence & Wishart, London.

Siim, Birthe (1988) Towards a Feminist Rethinking of the Welfare State. In K.B. Jones and A. G. Jinasdittir (eds) *The Political Interests of Gender: developing theory and research with a feminist face*. Sage, London.

Stacey, Margaret and Price, Marion (1981) *Women, Power and Politics*. Tavistock, London.

Vogel, Ursula (1989) *Is Citizenship Gender-Specific*. Paper for the Political Science Association, Warwick, 4-6 April 1989.

Whittick, Arnold (1979) *Woman into Citizen. The world movement towards the emancipation of women in the twentieth century with accounts of the International Alliance of Women, The League of Nations and the relevant organisations of United Nations*. Athenaeum with Frederick Miller, London.

Young, Iris Marion (1989) Polity and Group Difference. A Critique of the Ideal of Universal Citizenship. *Ethics*, **99**, Jan 89, pp. 250-274.

Young, Iris Marion (1990) *Justice and the Politics of Difference*. Princeton U.P., Princeton.

3

Gunilla Bradley

Psychosocial environment and the information age

3.1 Introduction

Integration between computer technology and telecommunications equipment has an effect on the design of occupational roles and our roles as citizens as well as on new patterns of how these human roles will be integrated.

The task of setting new goals and finding routes to reach these goals in the development of the information society is indeed important. Otherwise there is a risk that we will be stranded with an outdated industrial society implanted with robots, personal computers, visual display terminals, etc. In a step-by-step development there is still a risk of too much societal "patch-work" in a society that evolved as a result of another technology with other preconditions.

In the future computers with telecommunications - sometimes named "telematics" - will be the agents of social change. Telematics could be classified, for example, in terms of:

- "Productics": Computers, industrial robots and teletechnology.
- "Bureaucratics": Office information systems and teletechnology.
- "Privatics": Personal computers in the home and teletechnology.
- "Videomatics": Graphics, AV and telematics.
- "Visionics": Integration of videotechnology, robots and optics to create artificial "computer eyes" (Drambo, 1986).

New integrations will certainly follow in this ever-expanding field of information technology (Nora & Minc, 1978).

The communication structure will spread and influence all other structures in society and interact with them. Possibilities for totally new routes of development in society, in public as well as private life, will emerge as a result. Individual capacity for flexibility and opportunities for human competence building and skills development is crucial in this development.

There is a need for empowerment of the individual as well as for political systems that allow self-determination and imply a deepening of democracy. There is always a problem to find a balance between responsibility, rights and duties of the individual on one hand, and on the other hand at the organisational and societal level.

3.2 Computers, psychosocial work environment, and stress: from theory to actions

3.2.1 Summary of a theoretical framework

The RAM program was an interdisciplinary research program initiated and led by Bradley at Stockholm University 1974 - 1988. A theoretical framework was developed which was summarised in one model that included theoretical concepts. Their interrelationship were specified in a second model. The two models were empirically tested in three large work organisations in Sweden (see below).

The theoretical framework addresses:

- different levels of analysis;
- objective-subjective work environments;
- interplay between levels;
- interplay between objective-subjective work environments;
- interplay between working life and private life;
- life cycle perspective.

Figure 1 is one "application" of the theoretical framework especially addressing "stress".

The concept of **psychosocial** refers to the process involving the interaction between the objective environment and the subjective one. Essential concepts within the psychosocial work environment include factors such as: contact patterns and communication; organisational structure and design; work content and work load; participation in decision making; promotional and development patterns; salary conditions and working hours. In the Anglo-Saxon use of the word there is more emphasis on the individual and characteristics of the individual, which sometimes can be misleading. Anyhow I keep to the use of the concept with the definition it is given in Sweden and in the Nordic countries during recent years in laws and agreements. I also refer to the theory supporting this definition.

The term **psychosocial work environment** is used to signify the course of events or the process that occurs when objective factors in the environment are reflected in the individual's perception (either positive or negative) of work

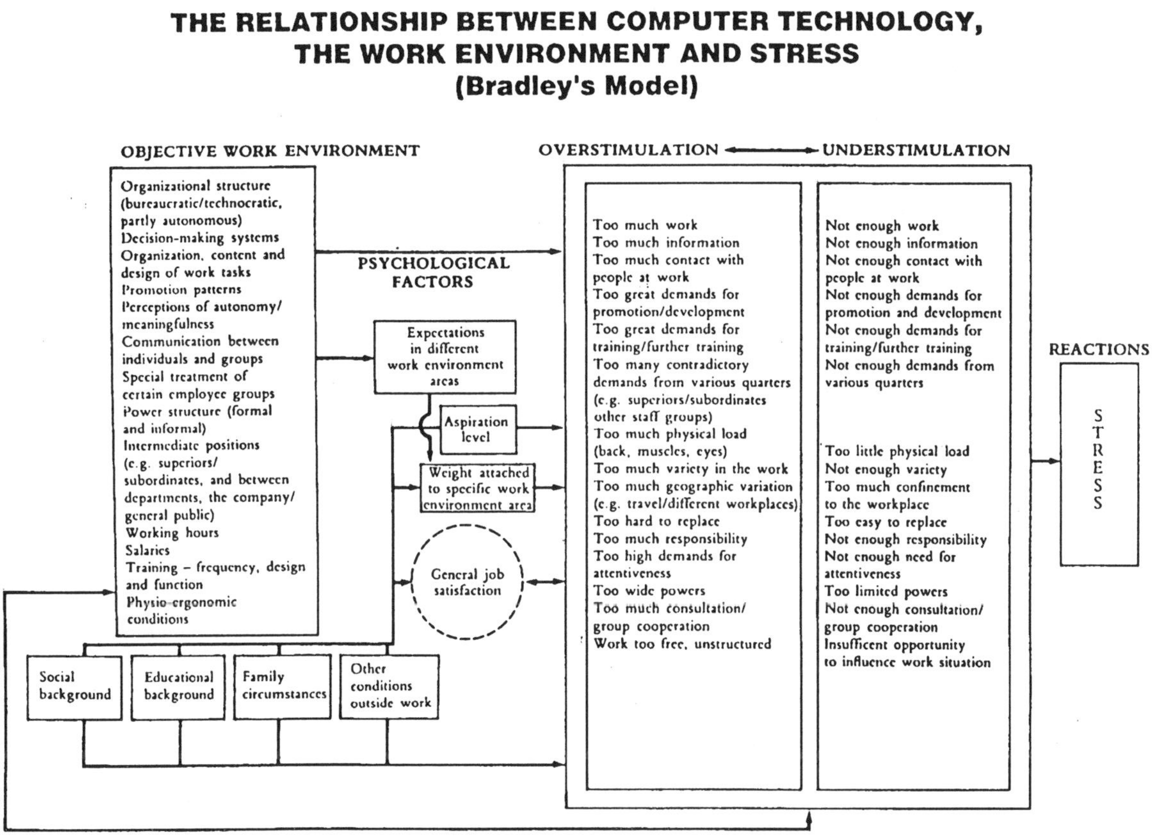

Figure 1: *Theoretical model*
Source: Bradley, 1977; 1989a

and conditions of work. Its essence is the interaction between the environment and the individual. Thus work environment factors exist at different levels - the level of society, the level of the company and the level of the individual - and they interact with one another. But there is also a distinction between the objective and the subjective work environment, which also interact (Bradley, 1989a, p.34).

The content of some of the concepts expressed in the models may be summarised as follows. The **objective work environment** refers to areas of work that are germane to large groups of employees. The **subjective work environment** consists of perceptions and attitudes related to corresponding sets of factors in the objective work environment. The subjective work environment is closely linked to the concept of job satisfaction. **The organisational structure** includes the methods used to allocate work, the basis for decision-making and organisational aids. Organisational structure is seen as an important part of the work environment.

Objective conditions outside work refers to behaviour and consumption, the conditions that prevail during the hours spent away from work. These may be affected by change related to the use of computerisation at work. Certain attitudes, values and experiences related to private life/leisure and family life were also analysed against the background of the introduction of computer technology into the individual's work.

Psychological variables is a general term covering a number of intermediate, psychologically relevant variables such as the level of aspiration and the weight attached to specific work environment areas. These variables are essential if one wishes to understand and explain the subjective work environment and its dynamics, and the perception of the conditions that govern our lives in general. They are crucial in the analysis of subgroups of employees and cultural variations.

The models used in the RAM program can also be used as theoretical models in discussing the **structure** which a computerised society should have (see the two-way arrows in Figures 1), and what might be **desirable goals.**

Within the research program the overall hypothesis was that different data-processing systems offer different conditions for the structure of organisations and the psychosocial work environment. Three main types of data-processing systems were studied during the RAM program. These three systems types are related to three phases in the history of computer technology:

1. a batch-processing system at a state-owned company;
2. an on line system with display terminals at an insurance company;
3. a microcomputer system at an electronic company.

Problem areas concern computerisation in working life. Essential concepts, derived from the theoretical models and developed in the research programme, were used to study the following: general questions about the work environment; information and participation in decision-making; organisational design, work content and work load; promotional and development patterns; contact patterns and communications; salary conditions and working hours; education and training; evaluation of work roles; physio-ergonomic conditions; leisure time and health. Regarding the quantitative analyses, 40 index measures of Likert type were constructed from an instrument including 300 questions.

The models illustrate a view of working life and its processes. However, there is a risk that the same phenomenon that occurs in working life in general - the fragmentation of knowledge - will also occur in the field of data-processing research and research into the consequences of computerisation. Integration is easily lost and it becomes increasingly difficult to gain an overview of the research results in terms of computer technology and various combinations of new technology. Parts of the reality can be separated out and described in great detail - effects can be shown - but the force of these effects in the interplay with other parts and "fragments" is often uncertain.

(Atomisation versus the holistic approach has always been one of the dilemmas of research, but becomes a more serious consideration in some disciplines. Artificial intelligence (AI) research is one example where problems arise when too limited theories about humans are applied and where there is a lack of interdisciplinary contact.)

Theories, methods and results from the RAM program are summarised in the book *Computers and the Psychosocial Work Environment* (Bradley, 1989a). In an on-going project a fourth phase of the computerisation process is focused upon, namely the use of knowledge-based computer systems (KBS). (See section 3.3.4 below.)

3.2.2 Action strategies according to the theory

According to the theoretical framework, people are affected by factors at national, company/organisational and individual levels, factors that the individual may also influence. These different levels may also feature discussion of action to be taken at computerisation. What do the state, the company, the trade union and the individual do to improve work and work content when computers are introduced, and what action can be taken? On the basis of action already in progress in the field of computerisation and the work environment, measures that should be given special consideration in the future will be considered.

Actions at the national level

One of the most complex labour market issues in Sweden during the 1970s was employee participation in decision-making at the workplace. A long series of changes and innovations took place. Three different levels of participation are usually mentioned: shop-floor participation, company participation and financial participation. (Corresponding index measures were used in the RAM studies.) Working systems are one area in which companies and government agencies have shown great interest. Some Swedish companies have attracted attention because of their efforts to improve the design of workplaces and job content, so as to create a better working environment and increase the opportunities for employees to influence their work situation.

A paragraph of the Co-Determination Act regulates the employer's primary duty to keep the employees informed about planned actions. Another paragraph defines the employer's duty to negotiate with the trade unions. These paragraphs have a specific relevance in the context of computerisation. The duty to negotiate spans a broad field, including various forms of computer use and problems connected to systems development. The Co-Determination Act has been supplemented by separate agreements.

The Working Environment Act was introduced in 1978. The concept of the working environment now encompasses work systems, work hours, and the physical, psychological and social adaption of work to human factors. Safety stewards (delegates) are guaranteed the right to halt dangerous work under certain circumstances.

The National Board of Occupational Safety and Health has given top priority to certain matters, one being computerisation in relation to working environments. Knowledge gained from research and general experience constitutes the basis of new laws and regulations, developed in cooperation with all the different interests involved in collective bargaining between employers and employees.

In the 1985 Government Bill on Informatics Policy, educational questions were given priority - at both basic and advanced levels. The Swedish Government allocated funds in 1984 to be used to attract more women into industry and the technical professions. The campaign was one step in a long-term plan to broaden the labour market for women. It is being conducted in project form throughout the country, using three approaches: measures for influencing girls' educational and professional choices, computer education/training for women, and recruitment and continued educational measures.

Actions at the organisational and individual levels

A major part of the current international debate on computerisation deals with the struggle for influence and power over the development of computer applications. Scientific reports and popular books analyse different strategies for system development (Docherty, 1977; Ehn & Sandberg, 1979). Theories have been presented with the aim of replacing, through a democratic process, the one-sided nature of planning and execution of rationalisation.

A parallel process involves identifying, structuring, describing and analysing work environment problems related to organisational and psychosocial matters. Awareness and recognition of work environment problems and their underlying causes are increasing. Desires and demands, expressed in actual programmes, are receiving wider attention.

People at work can present their preferences and requirements for the work environment when workplaces are computerised. General requirements may be laid down for an acceptable work environment, along with group-based requirements for a particular industry, a particular trade union, etc. Checklists may be used to elicit suggestions on which environmental issues should be considered, during the process of computerisation. Questionnaires or interviews may be used to evaluate planned computer systems or systems already in operation.

When data processing is introduced at their workplaces, workers must express their wishes, as individuals, for future development. They must be able to answer questions such as:

- what are the desirable characteristics of a good work environment?
- what is the desirable content of their future professional roles?
- what conditions of life (leisure time, family life, social life outside what is now called work) do they wish to have in the future?

There is an *interaction* between different levels of the work environment. A number of instruments have been established. Conditions have been created at the national and corporate levels for broad action to improve the work itself to bring about corporate change, but it is up to workers themselves to transform their work and its content, both in term of desirable goals and ways in which they can work towards attaining these goals. This interplay is also an important factor when action is taken in this field. Just as important as the existence of laws and agreements is what people themselves as individuals attempt to achieve on the basis of these laws and agreements.

General demands on the organisational and psychosocial work environment were derived from the RAM project; they cover working pace, influence, development on the job, education/training, human contact and communication, information, intermediate position/buffer role, physical strain, replaceability/job security, extrinsic and intrinsic sex equality. Computerisation should also help to create work environments where as few individuals as possible are overstimulated or understimulated.

Referring to the overview of action on new technology and working life, the most challenging task is to find a balance between strategies at the different levels or 'branches in a tree of action', not least between efforts at the national level and individual level (see Figure 2).

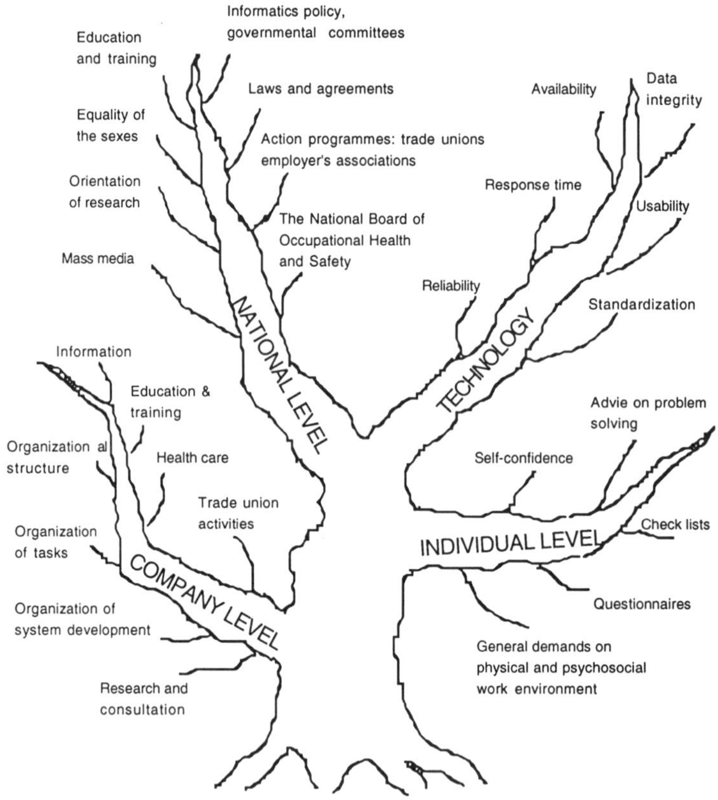

Figure 2: *Action strategies in Sweden - an overview*
Source: Bradley, 1986

Discussion

During many years there were prosperous experiences of the application of the so called "Swedish model", within the field of new technology and work organisation. However, that model is now debated intensively due to the economic and industrial structural development of the country as well as political change and reorientation in Europe and elsewhere. In this period of increasing market orientation, research experiences in the fields of psychosocial work and life Environment as well as organisational behaviour in general can contribute to strengthening the positive experience gained, and can contribute to creative thinking regarding structure and quality of working life and private life and our roles as citizens in the future.

The RAM project contributed with an awareness of the psychosocial work environment and its relation to changes in computer technology. The term "psychosocial" was built into the Swedish Work Environment Act where there also are certain paragraphs handling introduction and use of technology. Laws cannot be changed that easily even if changes in politics have taken place. I see signs today that the psychosocial work environment issues which primarily were driven by trade unions and their central federations are now driven from the employers' side and moreover in a more decentralised way. This is reflected, for example, in the orientation of new research funding.

The conclusions from RAM are still valid. Our emphasis in RAM was very much on psychosocial changes in the workplace at computerisation and how to handle those changes. A real interest for this type of research is coming from computer scientists, computer professionals and people involved in organisational changes in companies.

For the future I think we should not focus on formal issues of power and influence without developing ideas on how they should be used. We must maintain visions about the desirable workplace and society.

3.2.3 Stress and computers

In the following I will summarise some research findings and reflections derived from my research in working life. However, many of these issues are transformable to other sectors in life.

The introduction of computer technology appears to stimulate the creation of roles in working life and in private life that are characterised by either understimulation or overstimulation. Empirical findings supporting this stem from the three phases of computerisation; batch-processing systems, on-line systems with display terminals, microcomputerisation (Bradley, 1987).

A computer system should help to create tasks and work situations in which as few people as possible are overstimulated or understimulated. This must be an individual subjective assessment. Ideas have been put forward for a society of moderation and perhaps we should start to think more about moderation at our workplaces and in our homes; about environments that avoid extremes, where individuals suffer from too much or too little of the aspects that make up the psychosocial environment and that nullify the extremes of the opposing pairs (over- and under-stimulation). There are both quantitative and qualitative aspects to overstimulation and understimulation. One quantitative aspect in working life is the amount of work to be completed per unit of time, while the complexity of the work, for example, is a qualitative aspect.

There is a risk that the future labour market will have one group of highly qualified, highly educated people who are difficult to replace, and a second group with very low qualifications and high degree of interchangeability. The gulf between these groups will tend to widen. A third group, consisting of people not gainfully employed, "marginalised groups" or "fringe groups" will increase, and the rate of this increase will depend on how we conduct the inevitable overall long-term restructuring of our society as a computer society (Bradley, 1989a).

The following are reasons why work tasks and work environments that may expose people to one of the two poles of overstimulation and understimulation should be avoided in our society:

- the risk of stress reaction (the individual level);
- the risk of a fragmented labour force (group/organisation levels);
- the risk of exclusion from the mainstream of society (individual, group and societal levels).

Some types of stress that occur in display terminal work can be counteracted with technical aids - aids that affect response times, availability, screen layout, standardisation, etc. However, most stress problems have to do with work organisation and the psychosocial environment.

In the introduction of computer technology, not only the lateral division of work but also the vertical division of work must be considered when designing/changing work tasks and organising work to suit people's needs and aptitudes. In structuring professional roles when new technology is introduced, consideration should be given to several factors affecting job content. Attention should therefore be given to some questions of principle:

- what procedures apply in related professions at the same level in the organisation?
- what constitutes 'too much' or 'too little' at other levels?
- which tasks should be computerised and which tasks are better done by people?
- are there any work tasks that should not be computerised at all?

Research shows that co-determination in working life has an indirect effect on our role in the private life. Active roles in working life promotes an active orientation elsewhere - in citizenship roles.

In summary the inconsistencies between the needs of the individual, defined in one of the needs theories which are often discussed in human engineering, and the physical and psychosocial work environment, cause stress.

There is a risk that information technology or "telematics" enforces stress problems. When developing equipment attention should be paid to the user's role, to prevent stress at work or at home. Education and training could be used to learn how to prevent and "to cope" with inevitable stress phenomena in an information society. Special training is needed for risk groups. The actions cover many levels in the society (compare section 3.2.2).

3.2.4 Women and computers

Extrinsic equality is closely connected to the question of work division; a central aim is to obtain an equal distribution between men and women in positions in the labour market and in private life and, most importantly, in positions that imply power and influence. In this context, it is of great importance to watch the vertical and horizontal distribution between the sexes with regard to occupation, professional structure, and work division.

Intrinsic equality refers to men and women as a whole and as carriers of special cultures. The aim here is that the experiences, values, life styles, approaches, etc., which traditionally belong to women should have equal influence on social life in various aspects; so-called female culture should be utilised and preserved in the formation of our future society. It is important to consider psychosocial aspects of the work environment, and the balance between working life and private life/family life/social life.

The effects of computerisation go beyond employment and occupational structures. They also change the work environment itself, causing among other things qualitative changes in job content and in the relationship between work and leisure time/private life. Computerisation affects both the extrinsic and intrinsic aspects of equality. It thus is important that technological change in the field of data processing be monitored by bodies that deal with equality issues at both national and corporate/local levels and also at the level of individual women who go out to work and those who work in the home. It may be that a high degree of awareness of current trends will change the habits of women as a group so that instead of being mere 'observers' of technological change, they begin to occupy positions where they can exercise control and where technology becomes a means of supporting the striving of both women and men for equality at work and in private life. At the first IFIP conference on "Women and Computerisation" in 1984 in Riva del Sol I suggested a ten-point strategy for increasing women's influence in the area of computerisation and for changing their conditions of work and life.

Awareness and recognition of environment-related problems at work and at home and their underlying causes are gradually spreading. Interest expressed in action programmes is meeting with a broader response. Anxiety has been expressed that if the debate on computerisation is conducted strictly as a power issue, we will merely have a change of elite, or possibly create simultaneous elites. The issue of power is a crucial one, but power must be given a meaning reaching far down the ranks at our places of work. An understanding of the interplay of individuals, organisations, and society is just as important as a knowledge of programming and systems analysis.

3.3 Organisational communication and computer technology

3.3.1 Communication - one aspect of the psychosocial environment

Global economy and global networking has made new types of interactions possible, creating new business and collaborative structures in conjunction with changed production and the use of computer and telecommunication technology. Further, this technology is becoming all the more invisible or "transparent". Thus as a consequence of computer technology, especially the development of the micro-chip, computers have become more compact. They are automatically built into new equipment to the point that we no longer directly observe it ourselves. The results of these processes are changing the dynamics of the way our world functions. For example, as the countries within the "Pacific Rim" draw closer together, intercontinental contacts within some organisations become closer than those which exist between colleagues in their own countries or even those within their own workplace. In Europe, borders are falling as countries integrate themselves into the European Community. These types of broader questions must be understood since they also influence our frame of reference for communication between individuals.

Certainly, each of the five categories of communication must adapt to these new technological demands:

- within the individual - cognitive processes;
- between individuals, face-to-face communication;
- between groups/organisations;
- between individual and society;
- between reciprocal groups.

Each level is dependent on the technological communications level.

3.3.2 Communication and computerisation

In working life communication between people is greatly affected by technological changes, especially computerisation. This is also true for our roles in private life during leisure time. The process of change related to computer technology affects communication **directly**, according to the purpose of the data-processing system. This is obvious in the case when the operator is in direct connection with some type of equipment. Computer technology also has **indirect effects** on communication. This technology influences factors such as the structure of work organisation, professional roles, work content, influence and power, working hours and career patterns. These factors are in turn influencing communication between people.

Computerisation of the work environment also places greater demands upon the social and emotional components of communication and makes visible the unique qualities of human - human communication. Many of us have not adjusted to the information society (computers and telematics). Thus, we need to look at the interaction of people at work from both a quantitative (i.e. number of human contacts) and qualitative perspective. The qualitative aspects of communication include such things as creativity, emotional involvement and opportunities for problem-solving, listening, respect and trust.

3.3.3 Future changes

Instead of going into the results I will focus on future changes. The following hypotheses concerning communication and knowledge-based systems (KBS) are derived from a pilot study in the USA (Bradley, 1989b). They have been tested in three Swedish companies at the forefront of using knowledge-based systems. When writing this passage I am still in the USA, the Silicon Valley area and Stanford University, to discuss the research results on the early use of KBS in Sweden. The next step is to confront key persons in Sweden with various alternatives for the introduction and use of KBS in working life and for our role as citizens[1].

- Human - human interaction will decrease when expert systems are in use. Human - computer interaction will be more common as a contact pattern because the opportunities to discuss issues with other people are built into the systems. Further, these effects on communication are not unique to the AI type of technology.
- The use of new graphical presentation techniques (computer and telematics) will make communication more powerful and make it possible to communicate with a high degree of information content and complexity.
- There will be an increasing need for cooperative patterns in the workplace to be able to handle KBS. Interdisciplinary and interdepartmental contacts will have to be increased. More generalists and synthesisers will be needed.
- The use of KBS together with the traditional use of computers and telematics in combination will strengthen organisational structures

---

1 The KBS project is financed by the Swedish Work Environment Fund.

characterised by networking, flexibility, an emphasis on the communicative aspects of the leadership role, and non-hierarchical structures.

- If KBS are very successful the "elite" will gradually diminish. In ten years' time, however, it will be difficult to find a "human" expert (a person instead of a system) in certain fields to communicate with when new KBS are developed.
- Some people are getting more control. "Others are just being strangers". The outcome depends upon gender, culture, language, educational background, age, etc.
- Computers can be used to communicate with people when face-to-face contact is not desirable because it would be unpleasant. Human contact can also upset the rhythm of working with the machine.
- Helpfulness or resistance to collaboration and communication in the development of KBS (e.g. as "expert") depends upon whether self-respect is built into the position in the hierarchy or the professional role.
- Six types of educational requirements will be very important to communication throughout the organisation. People will need to learn to work in teams. There will also be an emphasis on learning how to make decisions, to solve problems, and to plan. It will also become more important to understand the nature of women's and men's job tasks, as well as to learn to work "between cultures".

In the Scandinavian countries, for example Sweden, co-determination between employers and employees according to laws and agreements has to be considered in the new KBS. This requires that new work roles are created and agreed upon in conjunction with the introduction of new systems. In this way jobs could be enriched instead of being deskilled or eliminated. This requires, however, an understanding of the psychosocial and organisational issues at hand. In a broad sense, this will influence communication in the workplace.

3.3.4 Empirical experiences on communication and KBS

The following is a summary of the comments offered by employees in one Swedish company regarding the impact on communication when using KBS.

A. KBS *replaces* personal contact

Advantages:

- More **"effective"** communication:
  - help in relieving experts of telephone and e-mail queries,
  - unnecessary questions can be avoided,
  - knowledge is more accessible out "on the company front line"
- The accessible knowledge gives an overview
  - support for the end user,
  - more pedagogical,

- an educational tool.

- A more relevant and uniform message.
- Sometimes it is easier to communicate with a computer:
  - "you don't occupy an expert's **valuable time"**,
  - "you can **'play'** when learning",
  - "you are not afraid of asking **'stupid questions'**".
- One way to give **official feed back** to the end users.

Disadvantages:

- Hard to deal with uncertainty in the knowledge
  - much uncertainty is dealt with intuitively in human - human communication,
  - but on the other hand KBS clarify the problem with uncertainty.
- Valuable in communication between humans when **explaining** things.
- Valuable in communication between humans when giving help in **solving the problem.**
- The system can **not** serve as a **"ball fence"**.
- Less need for contact with central experts.

B. KBS *affects* communication pattern and personal contact (quantitatively, qualitatively, and structure)

In the graph - the communication circle - an attempt is made to summarise the main structural impact in the organisation of the use of knowledge based systems, which indirectly are effecting communication both quantitatively and qualitatively (see Figure 3).

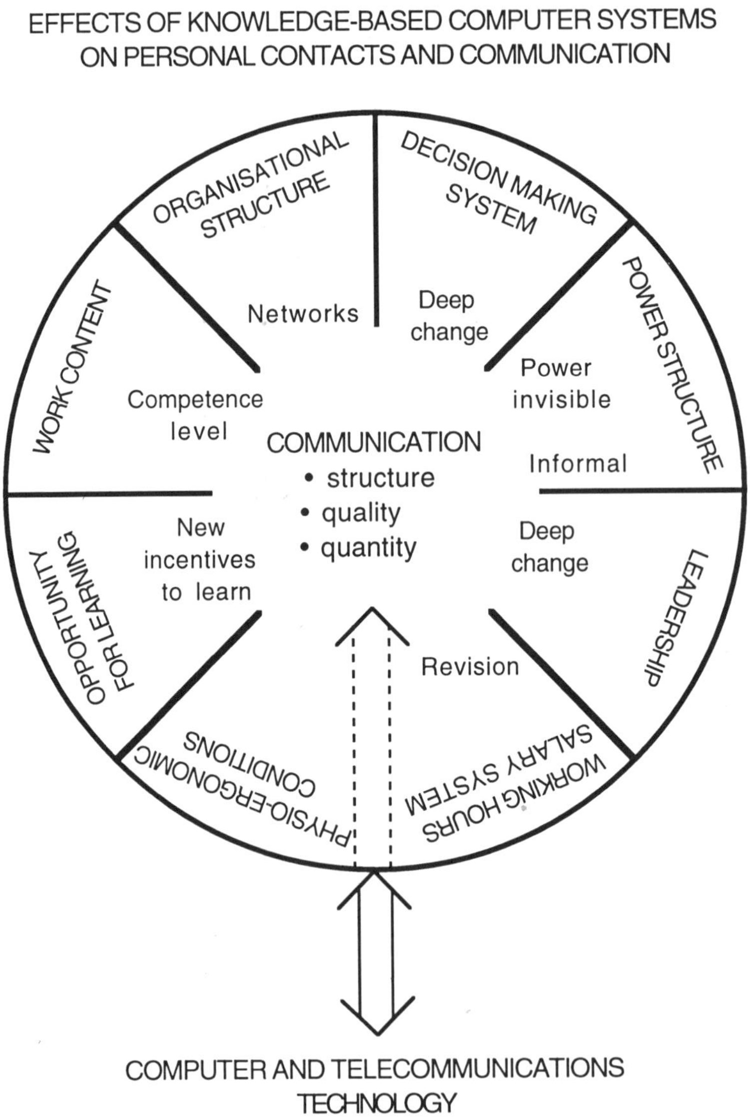

Figure 3: *Communication Circle*

3.3.5 Main trends (or hypotheses) on communication in the information society

In the following an overview of hypotheses is presented. They are being tested in a current research project that I am leading on Human Communication and Computers - Psychosocial aspects on the Individual and the Society in Change, financed by The Bank of Sweden Tercentenary Foundation.

- Information and communication technology effect our perception of time and space in a way that we perceive that we have less time and are "closer" to each other regarding space.
- There will be differences between subcultures and groups in the society due to educational background, sex, age and nationality.
- There is a change going on in the structure and quantity of the contacts and collaboration between people and in private life in the residence area and in the community. Electronic networks (electronic subcultures) are growing up in work and private life with various functions. There will be differences in the communications structure between different groups in society.
- Qualitative aspects of communication in working life (e.g. trust, security, confidence, interest, listening, emotional engagement) will be more essential. There will be differences between various groups. New dimensions in the quality of communication will occur.
- The balance between work, private life and family life is changing more and more. Private life will in the future assume a greater importance for people's need of contact and sense of belonging. A strengthening of traditional family life is taking place with few and close contacts.
- Electronic networks are strengthening the traditional division between male and female aspects in society. The electronic communication structure is changing the individual's self perception and identity.
- The subdivision between work and leisure will not have the same relevance in the future. Distance work and/or access to public databases at the work station (private services during working hours) are increasing.
- There will be a discussion about the extent to which lack of communication may be related to issues of knowledge and education, both regarding training at work and basic education.

Computer technology in working life has gained a lot of attention. The use of information technology for the development of **the role of citizens** is more limited. Within this field there is a big need for research.

The theses above may contribute to thoughts of how a computer-based communication system could empower and strengthen the qualities of the citizen's role, specified in section 3.4.2 below.

3.4 Conclusion

3.4.1 The allocation question

Whether seen in a national or an international perspective, whether focus is on our job role or citizen role, information technology entails a series of allocation questions. The list below was included in one of my first RAM reports and first presented in the Quality of Work Life Conference in 1981 in Canada. The issue of allocation is, more than ten years later, still relevant and might be more important as we approach an era where information technology interacts more deeply with our lives.

- Allocation of profit
  - between sectors within a country
  - between industrialised countries
  - between industrialised and third-world countries
- Allocation of work (shortening of working hours, division of labour, etc.)
  - allocation of leisure time
  - allocation of compulsory citizen services (paid and unpaid)
  - allocation of production and reproduction

3.4.2 Psychosocial citizenship

From our research on computerisation and the psychology of behaviour in many companies and organisations, I suggest some criteria for what could be entitled **psychosocial citizenship**:

- possibilities to influence one's own life conditions;
- possibilities for social belongingness;
- possibilities for a meaningful life content;
- possibilities for learning and developing oneself.

New organisational models for the relation between work, leisure and family will be discussed when the communication technology is used more in both work and private life.

3.4.3 Some questions according to the action tree

The action strategies were discussed at the Summer School in Brighton according to an action tree - an organic representation of a theory of action. The headings under "Action Strategies" according to the theory (section 3.4.2.2) were represented by the branches of the tree. We tried to answer questions such as the following:

What are the experiences in various countries?

What actions at these levels are going on in various countries?

What are the main interplay and interactions?

What are the main controversies and contradictions?

Are there any branches or sub-branches that we have not yet identified?

How and at what level and/or branch must we collaborate?

We tried to work together and supplement our national trees by an international tree of action. We tried to identify the strategies of international actions. We inferred on each sub-branch examples on the positive side and on the negative side. Our aim was to strive for an information society that could be depicted as a tree of fruits for us all to share.

Addendum

Here are some comments from the discussion. Richard Griffiths commented, "Wonderful, with an organic representation of a theory. The fruits on the branches of the tree are falling down to the earth and together with the leaves give the soil more 'knowledge' and that knowledge goes up into the trunk of the tree and nurture the branches". Cecilia Bergström quoted the Bible Prov. 11:17,30 "The fruits of rightness is the tree of life".

References

Bradley, G. (1977). *Computer Technology, Working Life and Communication.* The Swedish Committee for Future Oriented Research. Liber. Stockholm (in Swedish).

Bradley, G. (1986). *Stress and Office Automation.* Teldok, Stockholm (In Swedish).

Bradley, G. (1987). Changing Roles in an Electronic Industry - Engineers using CAD system and Secretaries using word-processing system. In: Salvendy, Sauter & Hurrell (eds). *Social, Ergonomic and Stress Aspects of Work with Computers.* Elsevier Science Publishers B.V. Amsterdam.

Bradley, G. (1989a). *Computers and the Psychosocial Work Environment.* Taylor & Francis, London.

Bradley, G. (1989b). Knowledge based systems and Work Design. In: Haslegrave C M, Wilson J R, Corlett E N, Manenica I (eds) *Work Design in Practice.* Taylor & Francis, London.

Docherty, P. et al. (1977). *How to succeed in Systems Development.* EFI, Stockholm (In Swedish).

Drambo, L. (1986) Infotopia. *Visioner och vägval i informationssamhället.* Liber, Stockholm.

Ehn, P. and Sandberg, Å. (1979). *Company Management and Wage-Earner Power.* Prisma in cooperation with The Swedish Center for Working Life, Stockholm.

Nora, S. & Minc, A. (1978). *L'informatisation de la société: nouvelle informatique et nouvelle croissance.* La Documentation Francaise, Paris.

4

Tom Mangan

Overcoming Disability: a UK perspective

4.1 Introduction

When addressing the subject of Information Technology and Disability in the context of 'Social Citizenship' it becomes apparent that issues beyond information technology (IT) need to be explored. The purpose of this exercise is to put IT in perspective in terms of its potential as well as limitations in the way it can benefit severely disabled people.

To start, it is important to question the way we have built up our perceptions of people with disabilities and to focus upon some of the factors which have created these views. In particular, the role of the media and charities will be considered as well as the way disabled and non-disabled people have been educated or, should we say, segregated.

The enabling aspects of technology have been able to explode a few of the preconceived ideas we may have had of severely disabled people and have given them a degree of self esteem. However, provision of this type of technology from the statutory services is erratic.

The report concludes by summarising some of the key points raised which should be considered as issues that would offer disabled people **rights** and **not charity**.

4.2 "Modern Day Freak Show"

"We need your gifts to help spastic children": so reads a sign inside a Spastic Society charity shop. This is an example of the image of disabled people that is sometimes projected to the public. Other examples include:

(1) the collecting box in a shop, of a disabled child with a slot in its head;

(2) an advertising campaign that depicted a disabled child in the middle of a field and included a heart-rendering caption underneath, which reads, "he'd love to walk away from this poster too";

(3) a major charity that launched a publicity campaign around the representation of a deaf person behind the bars of a prison cell. It said, the deaf person is isolated and incapable of doing things, unable to

catch a bus without an interpreter.

Why do charities produce these images? Because they are in 'desperate' need of funds and they are competing with other charities. Also, to raise money from the public it generally is the image of a helpless individual that encourages people to empty their pockets. However, organisations of disabled people are not happy about this and feel that Charity TV marathons such as Children in Need and Telethon are examples of a "Modern Day Freak Show" and should be banned.

Many of our perceptions of people with severe disabilities are taken from the media. Few of us have experience of direct contact. Is it any wonder that non-disabled people have these negative impressions? Although the high-street charity box appears to be dying out, it is being replaced by a 1980s and 1990s phenomena, that is, groups of enthusiastic young people rattling charity boxes under people's noses at railway stations and outside high-street stores.

There is an opinion that the rights of disabled people are lost amongst the collecting boxes and fun runs of well-meaning but misguided individuals. Groups of disabled people believe that the money raised props up large charities that are not accountable to the majority of disabled people. In addition they employ an insignificant number of disabled people and so maintain the status quo, which is to keep disabled people as recipients of charity. But is this being unfair to large charities? Charities are now changing with the times and generally attempt to portray disabled people in a positive light. But you could then ask the question, what are the functions of the charities? Their work includes assessment, education, training and sheltered employment. If these are seen as essential services, why should they be put under a 'Charity Banner'? Can these services be offered any other way, perhaps by the Government? Should more disabled people be sought proactively to take on senior jobs within these charities?

Organisations of disabled people believe that the medical models of themselves assume that they are ill and that they need to be cured. This model is reinforced when techniques such as conductive education are introduced to enable motor-impaired children to function as nearly as normally as possible by encouraging them to walk. A similar scenario can be provided concerning deaf people who are sent to non-sign language schools and are encouraged to speak. Although I do not want to appear to be criticising these two techniques, they are illustrative of attempts to get the individual to aspire to the way society is structured to see "normality". This can introduce children at a very early age to develop negative self-images and in turn to undervalue their ability. It avoids the issue of apportioning responsibility to the education system for not supplying accessible education environments for everyone.

4.3 Integration

The education system comes into question when we look at the education of disabled people. In Section 2 of the 1981 Education Act it was required that

Local Education Authorities should send children with disabilities to mainstream schools. It included one proviso, however, that it should be compatible with efficient use of resources. Seven years later, 80% of children were still segregated. Many of the stereotyped impressions non-disabled people get of disabled people originate from their lack of interaction. This image is not challenged by keeping disabled children away from mainstream schools. The arguments against the provision of special schools includes: that it segregates part of a community which has a lot to offer; the curriculum is very small; it does not prepare a person for the real world; and it is focused on the physical or learning disabilities of an individual as opposed to the equipment they need to do a job. Some of these points may be unfair but it is generally felt that integrated education is the right approach as long as adequate resources are provided.

Perhaps these arguments are not justified because it is unrealistic to expect a society to have a high level of integration. But this argument is weakened when we take a look at the situation in Sweden where 80% of children have integrated education which starts in kindergarten.

4.4 Enabling technology

Technology has a role in offering a significant number of severely disabled people a degree of independence. There is a wide range of equipment available to enable a disabled person to access a computer. Take for instance a simple device such as a keyguard. It is a sheet of metal moulded to fit over a keyboard and includes a series of holes to access the keys. This type of aid helps a person who has a hand tremor and would find it difficult to press a key without mistakenly hitting another key. The keyguard allows the person to steady their arm by resting on the keyguard and hence to operate a key.

For a person who is unable to use a standard keyboard there is a selection of alternative input devices including switches. A variety of switches exist to take advantage of the person's most consistent movement. The different type of switches available include chin, knee, tongue, infra-red, eye movement, foot and hand switches. To enable a person to use a switch to access the computer, the keyboard is redrawn on the screen. Once the switch is activated the screen keyboard is turned on and with a couple of clicks of the switch, a character is selected from the screen keyboard. This screen emulation software is memory resident and can be used with most application software packages. Although using a switch may appear slow there are a few software utilities which can speed up the selection. For example, one can store addresses and common sentences in macros which can be called up by selecting a couple of characters. Also one can use predictive software which will guess the word you are trying to enter. With these utilities it is surprising how quickly one can type using a single switch.

A system which is popular amongst people who have a spinal injury and are paralysed from the neck down is "Headstart". This product was designed for use with the Apple Macintosh. The Headstart system simulates the movement of the mouse. An ultrasonic beam is emitted from a box which sits on top of the computer monitor. The signal is picked up by a receiver which is in the form of a telephonist's headset. As the person moves his or her head the cursor moves around the screen. An item is selected by using a suck/blow device. Similar to the switch system described earlier, this system also uses a software keyboard emulator.

Recent development in technology has enabled the use of speech input to be a realistic alternative to the keyboard. In fact, there are already over 30 speech recognition systems installed in industry which have enabled disabled people to gain employment.

The use of the computer not only enables one to obtain access to a wealth of software application packages but it is also used by severely disabled people in the home to gain a greater degree of independence. The "Possum PSU6" is an environmental control system which allows one to control household items such as stereos, television, doors, curtains, and lights. All of these items can be operated by using a switch to select from a menu on a monitor.

4.5 Access to technology - Part I

It would appear that the computer can be accessed by most disabled people. But as technology evolves so new problems arise. Take the case of the graphical user interface which is used on the Apple Macintosh machines and now, with the advent of 'Windows', is becoming popular on IBM compatible computers. The problem here is that blind people who normally use a screen reader software package with a speech synthesiser to read the screen under the DOS operating system, can no longer use this system under Windows. This is because DOS is a text-based system and Windows relies on the use of graphical information. There are products coming on the market to address this problem but they do not, as yet, offer a complete solution. One of the problems with the way systems are designed is that they are always developed for disabled people as an afterthought, that is, after the hardware or software has been developed. Many of the problems disabled people face with using a computer could be removed if their needs were taken into consideration at the design stage.

One piece of legislation from the USA which encourages this is Section 508 of the Rehabilitation Act of 1986. It mandates that as of September 1988, office automation products purchased by Government units must conform to a set of guidelines for access by disabled people. It states that any new computer equipment contract that the government places must have outlined in its specification literature a section on access to people with disabilities. The three main areas include input, output and documentation. The guidelines they must comply with includes the following.

(1) Capability to execute multiple keystrokes (for example, ctrl-alt-del) serially rather than simultaneously.

(2) Capability to adjust the keyboard repeat tolerances.

(3) Capability to emulate mouse input device movements from the keyboard.

(4) When a modified standard keyboard is not appropriate, the capability to connect and use an alternative input device should be made available.

(5) Capability to support a speech synthesiser.

(6) Capability to present visual equivalent to aural information.

(7) Upon request, user documentation should be available in ASCII text format (on disk) or in Braille.

Although this legislation is restricted to US Government departments it is worth noting that they are the largest purchaser of computer equipment in the world and hence computer software and hardware suppliers will be encouraged to adopt their criteria.

4.6 Access to technology - Part II

Making the computer functionally accessible is but one of the problems disabled people face in accessing the technology. Other considerations are, who pays for the equipment and where does one go for a functional assessment? Let us look at funding and what is available through the statutory services. If a computer is required for communication purposes, whether it is to write or to speak, help is at hand if you need it in the following situations: in employment, higher education, and to a lesser extent, for vocational training. In employment, there is no fixed limit that the Department of Employment will pay for equipment to enable a disabled person to gain work. In higher education disabled students can obtain a grant of £3,000 to pay for equipment. But this does leave a number of gaps in the provision of equipment: for example, in school education, further education, part-time higher education and for daily living purposes. It tends to be this last category where the greatest need is required, that is, those who do not have the opportunity to work because of the severity of their disability and the discrimination it brings. These are the people who have the least access to funds. For this group of people charity is the only alternative and a significant number of people turn to this potential avenue for funding.

Funding of the equipment is only part of the picture, another significant hurdle is finding out what equipment would be the most appropriate for a disabled person's needs. For instance if a person is paralysed from the neck down, what would be the most suitable access device for his/her needs? It could be a standard keyboard with a mouth stick, or an eye movement switch, or perhaps voice control. But how well do these access devices work with "off the shelf" software application packages and what is the most comfortable? To answer these questions the individual needs a functional assessment.

Let us look at the provision of functional assessments for the different age groups. For a child there are a few centres qualified to give assessments, but there is a six-month waiting list. In higher and further education, there is a network of centres, called Access Centres, that can provide guidance, but funding must be obtained to pay for an assessment. In a training and employment situation the Government's Employment Rehabilitation Centres can assist. Again the people that need the most help are severely disabled adults unable to gain employment. There is some assistance available from the Department of Health's Communication Aid Centres, but they generally deal with people with speech impairments.

Now let us look at a case where a person's equipment needs have been satisfied. For example, the case of a fictitious disabled person called, Scooter. He is 25 years old and paralysed from the neck down and has been offered a job from an 'enlightened' employer. The barriers Scooter now faces include the following:

(1) is the employer's building accessible for a wheelchair?
(2) is there a disabled toilet?
(3) who will be able to offer him personal assistance regarding feeding and toileting?
(4) many of his disability financial allowances will be suddenly cut.
(5) he will be unable to use most forms of public transport because of its inaccessibility and hence must find alternative travel.

This demonstrates some of the disincentives of finding employment for a person in Scooter's position.

4.7 Realising the potential

The way society is structured and the priorities it gives can be illustrated by the following example.

A university had been designing a robotic hand to assist disabled people. It had 'feeling' in its fingers and could grasp objects firmly but gently. It was a project which had struggled due to shortage of money. The work had received funding of £50,000 over 13 years. The situation changed when the Ministry of Defence believed that the robotic hand could be used to handle plutonium. Suddenly £250,000 was poured into the project.

It would be reasonable to question the priorities of society, because it appears that the social construction of society and various structures in society, handicap disabled people. The fact that essential services for disabled people are provided by charities begs the question, why this is so?

Disabled people are some way from receiving true citizenship. To begin to move in that direction the following topics should be debated:

(1) more proactive involvement by disabled people in organisations representing the needs of disabled people;
(2) anti-discrimination legislation, to improve access to buildings, public transport and employment opportunities;

(3) personal assistance at home and at work for people with severe disabilities;

(4) a proactive movement towards greater integration within schools, including the provision of adequate resources.

On the topic of technology, the following points need to be addressed:

(a) a similar piece of legislation as Section 508 for Europe;

(b) a review of the way the Government allocates funds for disabled people regarding IT;

(c) a review of the Government services on disability and IT.

From the above list I would say the most important point is the requirement to move to a more integrated environment. It is in schools that a lot of the myths and prejudices begin. Segregated education can deny disabled people equal opportunities later in life, but it also denies non-disabled people the humanising experience of living with disabled people.

Note

This paper is based on the series of workshops given by Geoff Busby and Tom Mangan at the Summer School.

5

Anton Reiter

Education in the field of information technology

5.1 Introduction

Seymour Papert[1] said in his keynote address at the international conference "Children in the information age" in Sofia, 1987:

> *So we are entering the computer future, but what will it be like? What sort of a world will it be? There's no shortage of experts, futurists, and prophets who are ready to tell us - only they don't agree. The Utopians promise us a new millennium, a wonderful world in which the computer will solve all our problems. The computer critics warn us of the dehumanising effect of too much exposure to machinery, and of disruption of employment in the workplace and the economy.* (Papert, 1987, pp.3-4)

Both modern societies in the industrialised world and developing countries are moving towards the so-called information age which is symbolised by the transition from an industrial society to an information-processing society (Bell, 1973; van Weert, 1991). Information and telecommunication technology play a vital role in economic, commercial, social and even classroom activities nowadays. Most serious is the fact that the informatisation of society seems to take place as a "cultural mutation" affecting not only life styles around the world (Vitalari, 1990) but also our way of thinking (Turkle, 1984). This information revolution is accompanied by a drastic decrease in computer prices together with exponential increases of capacity. The advent of the forthcoming fifth generation computer leaves little to add (Berleur and Brunnstein, 1990). It is a matter of fact that the New Information and

---

1 Seymour Papert created the programming language LOGO which has been used in a variety of educational research projects related to children's learning, and the learning of programming in particular. It should be noted that even though LOGO had been grouped as a crucial theme of the sessions of both at the 1985 and 1990 IFIP World Conference on Computers in Education, the interest in the LOGO environment seems to be decreasing. The ability to write simple computer programmes is now accorded less importance as standard software packages have become widely available.

Communication Technologies (NICT), in particular the computer, have already found their way into schools.

John Olson argues:

> *Some call the effects of microcomputers on schools a revolution. Revolution may seem a strong word to describe the advent of "educational computing". It isn't. Nothing before has so stirred schools into action. School systems, teachers, parents and children talk about computers as they never talked about programmed learning, educational television, open education ...* (Olson, 1988, p.1)

Governments in almost all developed countries have introduced computers into the educational system, *"an increasing number of parents are feeling more and more guilty if they do not buy a computer for their children"* - as Jacques Hebenstreit sarcastically mentioned (Hebenstreit, 1988, p.4). What is curently (1991) available to schools would have been unthinkable ten years ago. And while the technology advance in the field of microcomputer and new transmission technology continues - and is even accelerated by the convergence of several technologies[2] including satellite technology to produce even more powerful uses - educationalists and politicians have to accept that the demands for investing in educational hardware and software will go on. Even one of the greatest critics of computer science, namely Joseph Weizenbaum, said at the UNESCO Congress "Education and Informatics: Strengthening International Cooperation" in Paris in 1989:

> *Another reason given for installing a lot of computers in schools, ..., is that computers are everywhere and that it is very important for children to learn about computers because the world in which they grow will be full of computers. Almost every job will be somehow laced with computers and so they had better know about them.* (Weizenbaum, 1989, p.7)

Thus, on all sides, the computer is invading our lives, changing our human relations and our relationship with the world. There is no doubt that whether or not we use computers in our jobs or in private life the main thing is to become familiar with and acquire a knowledge of computing. In the information society of today a familiarisation with computers has become a fundamental need of the citizen.

5.2 The challenges of the information society

The expressions "information society", "post-industrial era" or the "age of the new technologies", which convey a certain vision of society have a equivocal meaning. The determining factor has been the creation, processing and

---

2 The newest technologies (e.g. interactive video, interactive compact disc, CD-ROM, two-way cable and satellite communication, viewdata and others) offer enormous possibilities to teachers and pupils; in regard to CD-ROM (see Baumbach, 1990).

transmission of information[3], which is now the crucial issue to modern society. Educationalists nowadays affirm that one of the major tasks of the future resides in a strict adaptation to technological evolution.

> *We are going to become an information society, overloaded with information, but with the chance of having technical information processing capacity at our disposal everywhere ...* (Haefner, 1981, p.526)

The information society is undoubtedly the product of the technological (r)evolution of the last two or three decades of the twentieth century. An enormous explosion in the volume of knowledge has taken place: almost 10,000 scientific articles are published every day. Scientific and technological information is growing at a rate of 13% a year. The time lag between scientific discoveries or technological innovations and their application is becoming very short. The importance of the service sector is growing in the economic structure of industrialised countries. An increasing proportion of the workforce is involved in creating, processing and transmitting information. On the other hand workers are replaced by robots and lose their jobs (Lehner and Reiter, 1991, p.3).

The penetrating nature[4] of the information carried by the so-called mass media has meanwhile changed habits and behaviour of individuals and society. Radio and satellite television enter homes at all hours every day of the year. It is difficult to give any predictions how far these trends will go, but because of the cultural implications of NICT as a whole a "dark side" making us vulnerable can also be seen: there is a strong fear among pedagogists that especially young people will be manipulated by the media resulting in: (a) a questioning of authority and enormous change in human relations within the family, the school and the place of work; (b) a change of mentality and ways of life; (c) an enormous change in young people's values. On the positive side it is argued that the mass information society involves an increasing communication between different cultures which will perhaps give rise to a global civilisation (Balle, 1989, pp.79).

Consequently education has to prepare pupils for this aspect of their future, it cannot assist by resisting or standing aside:

> *The important issue remains, then, to understand the modalities of growth of such information and to monitor its development so as to master the consequences ...*

---

3 The term "information" has been identified as the essential feature of production, consumption and exchange in a post-industrial era by economists and sociologists; see Bell, 1973.

4 The simplicity of the binary code gives an exceptionally high degree of flexibility, and its non-specialised nature makes its application possible in a large number of human activities, helping to overcome a number of constraints of time, space and power. Society is therefore fully penetrable by the new technologies.

The role and responsibility of education in this respect are indisputable. (OECD/CERI, 1986, p.11)

Schools have to play the role of the "attentive mediator" (Eraut, 1991, p.17) when distributing information through media. Pupils should learn to use, select, classify, interpret and also search for information. It is absolutely necessary to adopt a critical and discerning attitude towards all kinds of mass information and communication. Any further debate on the media and new technologies is justified by the inherent possibilities and dangers which are unavoidable. Without ignoring current trends we must develop and control them by making them serve human goals. In political terms it is important that everyone should be able to become a well informed citizen in all attainable fields at all times.

Most national policies treat media education separately from the use of computers in the curriculum. In Austria a decree published in 1989 affirmed that

Media Education is not a specific subject among others but a principle integrated in all subjects of the curriculum, to be applied whenever the opportunity arises. (Eraut, 1991, p.24)

So the major challenge of the information society is to prepare the younger generations for a world in which information linked to its processing and its communication will play a fundamental role. At the 1989 standing conference of the European ministers of education which was held by the Council of Europe in Istanbul, Turkey, the following was demanded:

Education should now take a more pro-active stance towards changes in society. The new information and communication technologies...should not be rejected but accommodated through a more critical approach based on the fundamental human values of personal choice, equity and protection of cultural life. (Eraut, 1991, p.xi)

A position between blind resistance to NICT and uncritical acceptance will be necessary in future.

5.3 The new education crisis

Despite of all the advances in NICT, educational systems are inadequate and often poorly adapted to the new developments, and the result is under-educated citizens unprepared for life:

In the United States approximately one third of all people up to 30 years old are what we call functionally illiterate. It's not that they cannot read, they can read street signs, they can undoubtedly write their own name but they cannot read operating instructions for machines for example. (Weizenbaum, 1989, p.5)

The Carnegie Council of Policy Studies stated the same: a third of young people being under-educated, under-employed and under-adapted, were therefore incapable of making their way in American society (Balle, 1989, p.88). That is why knowledge of NICT has become essential and computer illiteracy often places people in a position of inferiority. As mentioned before, new technology floods the entire world of work and invades our lives. A foreseeable consequence of the rapid change is that no one would be able to pursue the same occupation for all his or her working life. We will be forced to renew our skills (life-long learning). Everywhere large companies have spent huge sums retraining and training the employees in information technology. Indeed, the penetration of computers has been most successful in firms. Personal computers for instance are nowadays more common both in small firms and in large enterprises than electronic typewriters. In the United States there were estimated to be some 80 million computers on corporate desks in 1988, in Austria about 400,000 at the same time.

The main reason for using computers was and still is that the machines improve(d) productivity and access to information. On the other side big corporations exploit new technologies as educational and training tools in order to give their staff - and customers - easy and cost-effective access to training through computer-based training.

As the educational system is moving far too slowly towards information technology in general K. Haefner predicted an educational crisis already in the early beginnings of the eighties:

> *Since more and more information processing is being transferred from human brains into the information technology, the presented role of the educational system will be questioned.* (Haefner, 1981, p.525)

Looking ahead, Haefner suggested that many activities still performed by humans in 1982 would be taken over by technology in the future. Instead of human hands robots would manipulate materials. The low-cost/benefit ratio of information technology would make it possible to use automated production. Human activity would then be shifted into control activities. People would prefer technical information processing in professional as well as in private applications because it would be more economic, available around the clock, more reliable and much faster compared to human information handling. While the information technology industry is still fast moving, profitable, powerful and well funded, the education system is in comparison slow, inflexible and badly funded. Education would be forced to adapt quickly or it would run the risk of disqualifying people. But in the beginning of the eighties,

> *In education, however, politicians, administrators and teachers presently behave in the way as information technology does not exist at all. The overall goals of the public educational system have been basically unmodified for decades. It is still the intention of 99 percent of all curricula to educate the autonomous human brain as the sole source of information storage and information processing.* (Haefner, 1980, p.973)

The human brain has been challenged both by the growth of information technology and by information-processing systems. Humans as information processors are in fact often not needed anymore, since there is a growing choice of using information technology instead. As we know nowadays Haefner's "revolutionary" ideas with which he influenced politicians and educational policy makers in Germany, Austria and Switzerland to establish a NICT-related infrastructure within the educational system have been supported. The fact that the quantity of information now available no longer enables individuals to amass encyclopaedic knowledge is of growing importance. Instead of memorising the data it is often more important to find any kind of information whenever required, for example through databases. Locating information, however, is not enough: at least a higher cognitive process[5] has to be applied in order to construct solutions and make decisions.

Haefner's statements of the educational crisis caused by the penetration of information technology into economy and society contained recommendations on how to master this crisis:

- Understanding the situation

  We should try to understand the serious impact of IT on education as well as gain a proper understanding of the forthcoming changes. This means that in each country several commissions would have to analyse the impact and consequences of the information technology for all curricula, taking into consideration a proper anticipation of the development for the time horizons 1985, 1990 and 1995.

- Planning and testing new curricula which integrate IT

  Development and evaluation of new curricula accepting IT as it is used in industry and private life. New curricula would have to do two things:
  (a) to integrate the information technology anticipated, and
  (b) try to qualify students at all levels beyond the tasks of IT as a centralised facility or as a personal information and telecommunication system.

- Bringing IT into the classroom

  It would be further of the greatest importance to allow teachers, students and administrators to have hands-on experience in the classroom of representative devices and systems of IT. Education should give advice how IT can be used properly. A general introduction to IT would ensure understanding of and qualifications in IT.

- Teacher training

  In addition to a general acquaintance with IT, it would be important to train teachers so that they can make use of IT as a teaching aid, as

---

5 Since information technology is automating easing cognitive task first, what is left for human workers gets more complex and sophisticated; see Jensen and Nissen, 1987.

> problem-solving systems and as a motivational aid for the students. This training is critical. (Haefner, 1980, p.977)

Many educational systems, for example in Austria and Germany, undertook these steps proposed by K. Haefner and considered the task of the educational system from now on of being a general interface between humans and their informational environment.

> *Justification of funding in the next decade has to come at least partly from a new view of supporting a "human right" of being well educated. These has to be a new motion of educating humans per se, ...* (Haefner, 1981, p.530)

Education needed to pursue a set of IT-related objectives in order to serve the interests of individuals as well as society as a whole and to find an answer to the problems listed as follows.

- How to prepare people for life in a world in which many cognitive tasks are performed by IT?
- How to modify curricula in a way that they integrate and use IT?
- How to motivate people to learn, if they know that a high proportion of cognitive work will be done by information-processing machines anyway?
- How to find a balance between cognitive work done by humans and by machines?

5.4 Literacy in the information age

It is a matter of fact that the impact of IT did not happen just because technology was available but because strong forces were pushing its implementation forward. Nor was the computer invented just per se but, as history illustrates, first of all for military purposes. Consequently, much of what happens in education in the field of IT is in response to pressures from outside. These pressures for the rapid advance of IT in the last decade and a half exist in every country, they only differ in the degree to which they have influenced policies and strategies. One has come - as said - from the military; the other pressure has come from industry, commerce[6] and the employment market.

> *In response to these pressures, most of the developed countries started ambitious and costly programs in the beginning of the 80s. The programs differed in terms of their specific objectives and strategies of implementation.* (Duguet, 1989, p.284)

It was demanded that a responsive education system, thus, should provide young people with training adapted to these requirements from outside.

> *The education system needs to provide workers with an adequate basis for the later acquisition of new skills, and to facilitate the movement of*

---

6 The strategy of computer vendors has played an important role in persuading concerned parents that today's computerless child is the twenty-first century's drop out, see Gergely, 1986.

workers between industries, occupations and employers. This implies a more flexible response by the education authorities to the changing pattern of occupational skills, but above all a higher minimum threshold of competences for all young people if they are to compete in the fast-changing labour market. (OECD Report, 1988, p.16)

The need for long-term flexibility and a broa- based education is of great value in the information age and of course important for curriculum development. The term "computer literacy"[7] has often been used to describe a basic general education in computing in order to make pupils (and adults when retraining) aware of what will be a permanent aspect of their working lives (van Weert, 1987).

The most common understanding of "computer literacy" is probably the ability to operate and use the computer. (Lauterbach, 1987, p.86)

Pupils should be taught "to use the computer as a tool of everyday life" (Taylor and Aiken, 1991, p.11). They should regard computer technology not just as an educational discipline but above all as a series of applications, methods and approaches which make it possible to extend the boundaries of human thought and action. The following types of goals are essential elements in computer literacy in general (Lehner and Reiter, 1991, p.6; Berleur and Brunnstein, 1990, p.471; Eraut, 1991, p.32).

- Some knowledge and understanding of computers and their technology.
- The ability to use a few standard types of software.
- Some knowledge of computer applications and their use in a variety of contexts.
- Some knowledge and understanding of the current and future impact of computer's upon society.
- The ability to write some simple computer programs.

As mentioned under note (1) programming is of less importance in teaching computer literacy because of the availability of standard software. On the other hand, it is doubted that programming can enhance general cognitive skills as had been claimed by Papert, the inventor of the programming-language LOGO.[8]

---

7 It should be noted that the term "computer literacy" has no unique meaning in referring to the different approaches in order to establish a basic instruction in IT; see Duncan & Harris, 1985, in particular the stream "Computer Literacy", pp.676-715.

8 The decreasing meaning of the LOGO environment was expressed in a study in which it was found that 69% of sixth-grade LOGO programmers had memorised the commands that tell the computer to draw an 90° angle on the screen, but only 19% knew how to draw the same angle on paper; see Correa, 1989, p.158.

To believe that the use of any specific programming language can make people become creative is either a naive view or an overoptimistic view of mankind in general and of children in particular; ... (Hebenstreit, 1988, p.7)

The availability of user-friendly software makes it unnecessary to learn programming in order to use computers for a wide range of applications. Experts therefore often state that making every pupil learn to program means the same as requiring everyone who wants to learn to drive a car to take lessons in engine repair first (Correa, 1989, pp.157-8).

Many of the educational objectives of learning about computers can be acquired nowadays through using computers for learning, which is known as CAL (Computer Aided Learning). From my point of view, a clear distinction between learning about computers that ranges from elementary computer awareness to advanced studies of computer sciences and CAL should be made for curriculum definition approaches anyway. According to the basic aims of computer literacy I would like to summarise that schools must teach their pupils the use of computers without in any way trying to turn them into computer scientists. Nowadays the use of computers involves no more specialised knowledge than for example the average motorist has of mechanics.

Education in the society of information does not require profound specialised knowledge of microelectronics or informatics; rather, it should convey a fundamental understanding of how information and communication technologies, work, what they are used for and what they must not be used for. (Lehner and Reiter, 1991, p.4)

Or shall we believe Joseph Weizenbaum, who stated at the UNESCO Conference 1989 in Paris:

The mastery of one's own language (both in its written and oral forms) and the ability to think and express oneself, clearly and fluently is a far higher priority of the educational system of today than imparting knowledge about computers and their use. (Weizenbaum, 1989, p.4)

5.5 General approaches to implement IT

The attempts of countries to introduce IT into education during the past decade covered four main areas: purchase and distribution of hardware; development, purchase and distribution of software; teacher training, pre-service and in-service; and research and evaluation. Policies and practices mostly with government involvement differed from one country to another as well as educational goals which would guide any policy response to the challenges of information society. Last but not least, differences in priority caused certain problems, often by the factor "timing": the development of trained personnel, quality software and appropriate pedagogic knowledge took a lot of time. Even if appropriate hardware and software was available, this was not sufficient if teachers were not adequately prepared. Therefore future programmes have to be carefully designed and implemented.

According to P. Duguet's address at the UNESCO-conference 1989, even if specific policies and strategies for introducing computers and related information technologies into the schools of countries differed, common broad trends were apparent:

> *In particular, there is a shift from "restricted" policies intended to promote instruction in computer science and computer literacy towards "comprehensive" policies designed mainly to increase the effective use of computer based teaching and learning across the curriculum.* (Duguet, 1989, p.283)

One goal of the "restricted policy" was to introduce the teaching of computer science into vocational and upper secondary education in order to develop computer skills for the labour market. Another objective intended to teach computer literacy to all students at all other levels of education in order to provide them with a basic understanding of the method of functioning of computers and their impacts on society. Countries like Australia, Austria, Belgium, Germany, Greece, Ireland, Italy, Japan, the Netherlands, the Scandinavian countries, Switzerland and most states of the USA were in this group.

The "comprehensive" policies intended not only to promote the teaching of computer science but also and mainly to use IT to improve the teaching and learning process. The best examples of countries with "comprehensive" policies were France ("Informatique pour tous"-project), and the United Kingdom (Microelectronics Education Programme, MEP). Specific implementation strategies for the development and the use of hardware, software, teacher training and evaluation were necessary.

A change has been taking place towards such comprehensive programmes since the middle of the 1980s by changing the orientation of programmes as in Portugal (The MINERVA-Plan, 1985-1988), the Norwegian Programme of Action 1984-1988[9] and Spain (The ATENEA-Plan, 1985-1989) or by introducing entirely new programmes as in The Netherlands (The OBSTAP-Project 1989-1992), APEID, the Asia and Pacific Programme of Educational Development and Japan's National Policy and Programme (Duguet, 1989, p.285; Taylor and Aiken, 1991, p.2). The pedagogic objective was focused on the computer as a tool for teaching and learning.

The successes and failures of countries which have used IT in education for many years should be brought to the attention of less advanced countries,

---

9 The Norwegian Programme ot Action was externally evaluated by the OECD 1987 in many ways. One of the main achievements is considered that a growing number of teachers and educationalists are now accepting the computer as an important learning aid in education in general; see OECD/CERI, 1987.

including the developing countries[10]. Co-operation could take place in many ways. It would be worthwhile to try to identify which strategies could be transferred to other countries. Research is needed for demonstrating the real effectiveness of IT in enhancing the learning process. Research and evaluation are areas for international co-operation, in particular in the exploration of the effectiveness of different teaching and learning approaches. The results would be of great value to all countries.

It is assumed by many governmental programmes that the use of computers is justified at all levels of education, including the elementary one. Others have targeted the diffusion of IT mainly on secondary schools. In Austria, for example, there are no plans for a systematic introduction of informatics at elementary school (1st - 4th grade) at the moment even if several projects are running and are accompanied by scientific research on the subject.

> *This decision is founded on the argument that all pupils of those age groups should first be taught conventional cultural techniques whose knowledge remains indispensable for everyday life.* (Lehner and Reiter, 1991, p.16)

The question remains whether or not there are any benefits to be gained from the use of computers at an earlier educational stage. More common is the pattern of starting with the implementation at the higher level, to concentrate on higher education where an appropriate use of computers can probably be reached. Educationalists often expect an overall improvement of learning and working with computers (Schmidt, 1990; Mitzlaff and Wiederholt, 1990; Legat, 1988).

As a generalisation we can say that strategies used for implementing IT-related objectives into the curriculum, that computer literacy in the meaning of a familiarisation with informatics, and a real systematic introduction defined as computer science are

> *more widely apparent in the tertiary and secondary technical and vocational education than in primary and general secondary education and much more rarely in pre-school education, special education and adult education, ...* (UNESCO, 1989, p.22)

5.6 Evaluative research and findings

As previously mentioned, countries which have not yet made large investments in IT would have the opportunity to learn from existing experiences and failures in order to avoid costly but ineffective operations.

---

10 To bridge the gap between developed and developing countries international co-operation should be strengthened, i.e. in the production of software within the cultural contexts of the developed countries. Introduction of IT in the developed countries should start at the university level first and proceed downwards, involving the whole educational community with broader cooperation with industry; see Eraut, 1991, p.72.

Any approach of IT into the educational system needs to be planned carefully and appropriately funded. Beside investments in hardware and software, the human factor is very important and requires well designed and comprehensive training programmes. So far research and evaluation has been necessary to collect some evidence of what has been accomplished and successful. At the Conference of European Ministers in Istanbul, Turkey, 1989 the necessity of research and evaluation programmes as areas for a broadest international co-operation in particular in the explorations of the effectiveness of teaching and learning approaches was proposed (Eraut, 1991, p.68).

It is of course difficult to set definite goals through research and to use past experience for future projects in the educational field, because - as we know - both hardware and software become obsolete within a short time. Despite the factor of time in the area of IT which seems to paralyse educational systems and makes it impossible to make accurate predictions there are several reliable findings concerning teacher training, hardware and software issues. Research shows that the most successful implementation of computer education resulted in teacher training before consideration of suitable courseware and hardware.

5.6.1 Teacher training

Teacher training has been the crucial issue for any successful introduction of computers into schools. In most countries, hardware and software were delivered before teacher training had started (Duguet, 1989, p.288). The only successful strategy was to develop adequate pre-service modules. Since the middle of the 1980s teacher-training in IT has become compulsory for new teachers, while the experienced teachers, whose knowledge and skills should be up-dated through periodic education, very often attend voluntarily training programmes in IT. Life-long learning concerns teachers, too, which means that

> *all teachers need minimum skills to manage, use, adapt evaluate and consider computer use in specific teaching process.* (Gumbo, 1989, p.220/221)

Teachers must therefore be trained so that they see themselves as being in control of the technology. During an educational workshop on the theme "Interactive learning and the new technologies" in Eindhoven, The Netherlands, 1987, with the idea to put together research and experience to show in what way the new technologies had succeeded, it was assumed that

> *The majority of teachers have never seen the new technologies in action and are therefore sceptical as regards their usefulness. To train them will be a long-term task.* (Harrison, 1987, p.7)

One of the main remaining problems, thus, is teacher training. There is still a lack in adequate teacher training programmes to be established and a lack of competent and highly motivated teachers. So what is important for future of pre-service and in-service training? At the Eindhoven conference the following recommendations were given (Harrison, 1987, p.11):

- The orientation towards IT must be integrated within the curriculum as a whole.
- Inputs in training-programmes must come from pedagogy, psychology and computer science.
- An integrated approach towards all interactive technologies is necessary.
- Training should also be focused on the criteria for evaluating software.

As a conclusion for the future, we may demand that *"all teachers should be able to use computers for teaching purposes with the same ease as other teaching aids or audio-visual teaching."* (de Landsheere, 1991, pp.151-2).

5.6.2 Computers as educational tools

Several evaluative case studies indicate that in specific learning situations the use of microcomputers together with software applications produces positive results both in vocational and general education. The educational benefits of computers and various types of software as teaching and learning methods have often been demonstrated.

> *Computers can aid the teaching of existing subjects, or they can introduce students to whole new ways of learning.* (Olson, 1988, p.2)

Being the "teacher's aid in either case"[11] computers in the classroom have doubtless many potentials. They can (Olson, 1988, p.115):

- offer multiple representations and perform complex transformation of information,
- form bridges between different but related things,
- control the production of personal traces of what was done and store the results of accumulated effort.

Indeed, the potential use of computers as powerful instruments for supporting the teaching and learning process is considerable. But the uses of IT in schools obviously depend on the existence and distribution of software through which the possibilities opened up by computers can be fully exploited. The range of the available software is vast, from specialised software to tutorial programs via applications such as word processing, database and spreadsheet packages. But it is generally assumed that there is a lack of good quality software even in countries with a large diffusion of computers in schools. This lack of software and - as mentioned - of highly qualified teachers may reduce utilisation of IT in schools. One of the reasons is that the market for educational software is relatively small and strategies to increase its size in

[11] It should be noted that enthusiasm for computers is driven by research on microworlds based on the theories and yet unrealised promises of artificial intelligence, see Olson, 1988, p.6. But it may be doubted that the computer can eventually replace individual skills and individual creativity.

order to "encourage software producers to invest in powerful learning materials such as simulation and model building, program solving or exploration and discovery" (Duguet, 1989, pp.286-7) were not successful. Consequently quality software remains expensive while the market for it remains small. Therefore it was proposed at the EEC-conference 1989 both to promote standardisation in hardware, so that as many systems as possible can use the same software, and to make translations and adaptations of software from one language to another. A more intensive European co-operation should be necessary to reach this objective (Eraut, 1991, p.72; OECD, 1988).

On the other hand not only a small market is responsible for this lack of quality, it is often the low quality of the products available for use in schools. (Lehner and Reiter, 1991, p.54; Winship, 1989).

> *Out of more than 7,000 packages available in the United States, for instances, only about one in four were reported to meet minimum technical and instructional standards and only about three of four out of 100 were considered excellent.* (Correa, 1989, p.160)

While so-called "Drill and Practice" software has shown limited effectiveness, simulation software offers a useful means

> ... *simulation is useful in education because it allows experiments which would be too expensive or too dangerous or just impossible to make in the laboratory.* (Hebenstreit, 1988, p.8)

as well as classical application packages such as word processing, database and spreadsheets.

As teachers are often not aware of what software is available to them, many OECD countries have set up software information and evaluation centres in order to provide teachers with information about the quality level of available teacher and learning software (Duguet and Winship, 1990, p.68). Such agencies and centres exist for example in Australia (National Software Coordination Unit), Austria (EDP training Centres), Canada (Database of the Council of Ministers of Education), France (Educational Software Commission of the Ministry of Education), Germany (Institute of Science Education), Japan (Center for Research on Educational Software of the Ministry of Education), the UK (National Educational Resources Information Service) and in many other countries. Despite of the diversity of curricula, cultures and languages a closer (European) co-operation not only in software reviewing will be an essential goal for the future. It is also necessary to establish electronic databases in the field.

5.7 Information technology in Austrian education: a survey

The growing significance of information technology was taken into account in the Austrian education system at a relatively early stage (Reiter and Rieder, 1990; Fischer, 1988). The first preliminary attempts at incorporating electronic data processing into the school curricula took place towards the end of the 1960s and, in the following years, it became more and more widespread at different types of school.

The development of electronic data processing (EDP)/informatics in Austrian education was closely moulded on the classic approaches: the machine orientation of the late 1960s was replaced in the 1970s by the algorithm-orientated model of thought, which promoted the application of programming languages. Since the beginning of the 1980s it is the user-orientated approach that has been put to the fore in many cases in EDP/informatics. This approach sees people and society in a reciprocal relationship with the new technologies and emphasises the aspect of computers as a working tool. Today, the main concern of information technology education in Austria is to acquaint pupils with the new information and communication technologies in the course of their general education in such a way that they are able to use them in a purposeful way. In this process, they are shown to be the opportunities and the limitations of these technologies; groundless fears are to be dispelled at the same time as blind faith in technology is to be countered.

Basic education in information technology for all pupils in the 7th and 8th forms is continued into the 9th form at general high-level schools with the subject informatics and complemented at medium and high-level vocational schools with professional and application-orientated EDP knowledge. To help comply with the specialised job profiles that have emerged in EDP and informatics, vocational education offers a five-year education course at present at six high-level secondary schools for electronic data processing and organisation as well as the subject informatics, which is firmly established at several universities.

5.7.1 Basic education in information technology

At the start of the 1990/91 school year basic education in information and communications technologies (informations - und kommunikationstechnische Grundbildung, ITG) was introduced in Austria for pupils in the 7th and 8th forms. All pupils, boys and girls, now have direct access to the new technologies by the age of thirteen. The so-called "Integration Solution" was chosen as the means of anchoring this basic education. It includes teaching educational elements of informatics within the framework of existing school disciplines.

This integration not only complies with the holistic approach to information and communication technologies but also contributes towards reaching the objectives of basic education in information technology, as follows.

- Pupils are to gather their own experience with the new technologies in general and the computer in particular and in so doing acquire basic skills and abilities.

- They should be capable of analysing with a critical mind the experience acquired in the past and of situating it in a broader context.
- The newly acquired knowledge of information and communication technologies should first and foremost be of a general nature; specialist knowledge is not a priority.
- An essential element of ITG is to take into account the opportunities and the limitations of the new technologies, their effect on the individual person and the development within society as a whole.

In practice the Integration Concept provides for an introductory phase in the 3rd and 4th class of the "Hauptschule" (compulsory junior secondary general school) and the "AHS" (high-level general secondary school) (7th and 8th forms), with thorough preliminary information in the 7th form and a project phase in the 8th form. Computers are used according to the specific nature of the subject matter in the subjects German, English, mathematics and geometric drawing.

This basic education places special emphasis on affording boys and girls alike the same opportunities of access to the new information and communication technologies, irrespective of sex. In this connection it has to be taken into account that existing prejudices, which would have it that females are less gifted in technology than males, have in many instances already taken hold of EDP (Clark, 1990; Sanders, 1990; Schulz-Zander, 1990). For this reason the Federal Ministry of Education and the Arts has outlined an area of research on the social aspects of access to computers and on the matter of interactions in the classroom itself (BMUK, 1990).

An independent task force is working on drawing up proposals for ways in which to perceive and dismantle the sex-related obstacles that bar access to information and communication technologies.

5.7.2 Pedagogy for the education of handicapped children

Priority is given so that all children in Austria should receive the same opportunities to apply information technology. Handicapped and disabled pupils should be prepared for both private and professional use of computer-assisted learning and communication aids. There is an increasing use of the computer as a communication aid for helping children with a severe sensory impairment or a motor disability.

In addition there are also school pilot projects aimed at giving a fundamental education in information technology, taking into account the individual abilities and development of the handicapped child.

5.7.3 Hardware and software facilities at general schools

To implement the Integration Concept a second classroom with 15 AT computers (14 286-microprocessor based pupil workplaces /1 teacher workplace on a 386-basis, VGA monitor) and laser and/or matrix printer(s) had been set up at 189 state AHS by the 1990/91 school year. Most of the state AHS schools have opted in favour of a network variant (Novell network), which offers a number of advantages for instruction. A videotext workplace is also part of the basic AHS equipment. By the 1990/91 school year the 1,200 "Hauptschulen" (compulsory junior secondary general schools) had acquired between 6 and 8 computers per school location.

In terms of software a basic package comprising word processing, spreadsheet and CAD (Computer-Aided-Design) programs has been compiled for the general secondary schools to be used in German, English, mathematics and geometric drawing. This basic equipment also includes an integrated package. Over the next few years the equipment standard at AHS schools is to be extended with PCs specially geared for the subjects of physics, chemistry, music and sculptural education. Compulsory junior secondary schools are also aiming to expand their present facilities.

5.7.4 Informatics at the second cycle of the AHS (5th-8th class)

With the coming into effect of the reformed second cycle of the AHS during the 1989/90 school year, informatics as an existing practical subject became a two-year compulsory subject. Instruction is aimed essentially at teaching the uses of application software and at working out structured problem solutions taking into account the general laws on which information processing is based. The social aspects of EDP uses are also explored. In the 6th, 7th and 8th classes of the AHS, informatics is available as an elective compulsory subject and as an optional subject. In this way existing knowledge and skills can be improved and additional knowledge gained. In many cases instruction is project-orientated.

5.7.5 Informatics at the "Polytechnischer Lehrgang" (Prevocational School)

The purpose of the "Polytechnischer Lehrgang" is to prepare pupils for their professional careers upon completion of the "Hauptschule" or the first cycle of the AHS. Here again, special emphasis is placed on informatics. Since the 1989/90 school year pupils at the "Polytechnischer Lehrgang" are also given instruction in informatics as part of one of the seminars of their choice (the choice consisting of social studies and biology, economics, natural science/technology and agricultural science). Informatics as a subject of instruction is also part of the alternative compulsory subjects such as bookkeeping or typing, and is also taught as an optional subject with one to two hours a week.

5.7.6 EDP at medium and high-level vocational schools

Practical considerations are the main priority for EDP education at the vocational schools. At the technical and trade schools for instance, CAD instruction is a priority subject along with the compulsory subject "EDP and applied EDP" while at medium and high-level business schools the use of EDP in the commercial area is a focal point of instruction.

At the high-level vocational schools for humane studies (secondary schools for domestic science, tourism as well as fashion and clothing techniques), EDP is incorporated as a main point of emphasis in the subjects "accounting", "stenotyping and word processing" and as practical subjects in practical company courses at the secondary schools for tourism and catering or the practical application of the newly developed data technologies for the textile industry: CAD, computer-aided cutting design and cut-layout optimisation.

At the high-level secondary schools for agriculture and forestry, EDP instruction aims to familiarise pupils with the function, organisation and purpose of EDP installations.

The subject-specific use of EDP in medium and high-level vocational education in Austria is rounded off by syllabus adaptations aimed at strengthening, also at vocational schools, the instruction in EDP knowledge and handling that is necessary for the vocation concerned.

5.7.7 Training, advanced training and further training

In the course of their studies at teacher-training colleges, future teachers of elementary schools, compulsory junior secondary general schools and special schools are given an insight into the new information technologies; they learn how to use them in practice and how to develop possible useful applications in classroom. The optional subject "Informatics" is available for those wanting to acquire an additional qualification.

The specific EDP/information training requirements for teachers at vocational schools who do not have university or college education are provided by the vocational teacher-training colleges. Most of the advanced teacher training for high-level general schools and the vocational medium and high-level schools is taught by the teacher training colleges. At EDP/informatics courses lasting several semesters they continue to provide teacher training until a sufficient number of teachers with university informatics education are available.

At present certain universities offer the possibility of acquiring, as a university course, the qualification to integrate computer instruction in the teacher's specific subject. Work is currently in progress on drawing up a general regulation for university education in informatics for candidates to the teaching profession.

5.7.8 Information and training centres

Throughout Austria there are a number of information centres offering interested pupils, teachers and parents the opportunity to try out and compare various computer models and programs. These centres are also available for training and advance training purposes as part of adult education programs.

5.8 Computers in the daily life of Austrian schoolchildren

At the start of 1991 the sociologist Dr Walburga Gáspár-Ruppert submitted a scientific study entitled "Die Spaß-Maschine. Der Computer im Alltag österreichischer Schüler/innen" (Fun Machines - Computers in the Daily Lives of Austrian Schoolchildren) which offers interesting insights into the attitude of youths of both sexes to computers (Gáspár-Ruppert, 1991). Overall Gáspár-Ruppert came to a very enlightening result as regards the attitude of schoolchildren to computers. Indeed, her findings have shown that for the majority of schoolchildren of both sexes, computers are primarily an interesting and, compared with other instruments, extremely flexible "toy-cum-tool". While the interesting aspect is further strengthened by informatics lessons at school, in most cases the initial contact with computers usually takes place before tuition is given at school.

The study also revealed that the fact of installing a computer in a child's room is by no means a way for concerned parents to keep their child happy at all costs; indeed, in nearly all of the cases it was the children themselves who asked for the computers to satisfy their curiosity and their craving for "novelties".

Noticeable differences in the attitude objectives in relation to age are due to a large extent to the fact that among the lower age groups the novelty of the computer results in a more intensive involvement with it. The main incentives for schoolchildren, children and youths are curiosity, play and risk-free trial and error. Sometimes there are also instances where children experience a sensation of power as a result of "dominating" a machine.

A direct consequence of "instrumental competence" is the prestige that appears within a group of friends whenever a child or youth becomes expert at handling computers. However, it has been shown that the appeal of computers wanes the more it is integrated in the daily lives of young people. As instrumental competence increases with age and as activities adapt more and more to future careers, computers lose their function as toys or games to become professional tools, which in general are no longer fun. According to the study conducted by Gáspár-Ruppert this is primarily a pragmatic decision on the part of the adult-to-be and not a quality inherent to the computer.

Sex-related differences were also identifiable in the survey. However, they cannot be attributed to the fact that girls are less interested in or not as competent with computers "by nature". Rather, family conditions play an essential role in shaping their behavioural patterns. Girls are as uninhibited and as unprejudiced as boys in their attitude towards computers provided their interest and their curiosity (which are as pronounced in girls as they are in boys), are stimulated and promoted accordingly. It could well be a sign of frustration if girls lose interest quicker than boys. In this case it can only mean that less is done to satisfy the requirements of girls. Possibly another factor is that girls attribute less importance to computers for their future professional activities than boys do.

The material collected from the questionnaires does not support the assumption that involvement with computers at school and at home will give rise to a generation of "compulsive programmers". Nor are there any indications that computer technology is causing a loss of social competence; on the contrary, by virtue of its toy or game character, it can even promote and considerably strengthen contacts between children of the same age. A possible withdrawal from social relationships might occur in the case of socially and/or psychologically impaired children; however, the appropriate data is not available at present to substantiate any such claims.

The usually effortless processes of habituation and adaptation, among schoolchildren and children in general should not however conceal the fact that there might be repercussions in the longer term that it is not possible to assess at present. For this reason it is essential that the possible consequences and effects of using computers be discussed and processed, as is intended by the school curricula. Whenever possible it is not just the social aspect as a whole as stipulated by the curricula - but also the psychological and psycho-social area that should be integrated. Under these prerequisites the teaching body should in future devote special attention to the clear difference in behavioural patterns among children of the lower age groups; certainly it would seem that parents have not yet been able to acquire a sufficient degree of competence to assume tasks such as these, which imply a very intensive involvement with computer technology.

5.9 Conclusion

The objective of this contribution was to concentrate on the subject of education in the information age. Information technology is growing in importance for modern educational curricula. The complex area of multimedia and the field of telecommunications are just two new branches which will revolutionise the teaching and learning environment in the near future. Educationalists should always have their visions even if there is as yet not much sign of the predicted classroom revolution that teachers would be replaced by computers - which is of course still as fanciful as it always was. I would like to close with a statement of Tom Forester's address to the participants of the seminar "What ever happened to the Information Society?" at the Gottlieb Duttweiler Institute in Zürich in October 1991:

> *The truth is that society has not changed very much. The microchip has had much less social impact than almost everyone predicted. All the talk about "future shocks", "third waves", "megatrends" and "post-industrial" societies must now be taken with a large pinch of salt. Life goes on for the vast majority of people in much the same old way. Computers have infiltrated many areas of our social life, but they have not transformed it. Computers have proved to be useful tools-no more, no less. None of the more*

extreme predictions about the impact of computers on society have turned out to be correct. Neither Utopia nor Dystopia has arrived on Earth as a result of computerisation. (Forester, 1991, p.1-2).

References

Balle F. (1989) The Informatics Society, Schools and the Media. In: M. Eraut (1989) pp. 79-144.

Baumbach J. D. (1990) CD-ROM Information Sources for Students: Anticipated Outcomes and Unexpected Challenge. In: McDougall andDowling (1990) pp.19-23.

Bell D. (1973) *The coming of the post-industrial society.* Basic Books, New York.

Berleur J. & Brunnstein K. (1990) Recent technical developments: attitudes and paradigms. In: J. Berleur, A. Clement, R. Sizer & D. Whitehouse (eds) *Information Society: evolving landscapes.* Springer-Verlag, New York.

BMUK (1990) *MUT.* Mädchen und Technik, Wien.

Clark V.A. (1990) Girls and computing: dispelling myths and finding directions. In: McDougall & Dowling (1990) pp. 53-8.

Correa C. M. (1989) Informatics in education: objectives, requirements and costs. In: UNESCO (1989) pp. 157-62.

de Landsheere G. (1991) The Information Society and Education. In: M.Eraut (1991) pp.115-63.

Duguet P. (1989) National strategies and their extension to the international level. In: UNESCO (1989) pp. 283-90.

Duguet P. & Winship J. (1990) The quest for quality software. In: McDougall & Dowling (1990) pp. 67-72.

Duncan K. & Harris D. (Eds) (1985) *Proceedings of the IFIP TC3 4th World Conference on Computers in Education - WCCE 85.* North Holland, Amsterdam.

Eraut M. (ed.) (1991) *Education and the Information Society: a challenge for European Policy.* Cassell.

Fischer H. M. (ed.) (1988) *Österreichs Schule 2000. Computer, Informatik und neue Medien im Unterricht.* Stellungnahmen, Berichte, Konzeptionen, Graz: Leykam Verlag.

Forester T. (1991) *Whatever happened to the Information Society?* Keynote address at a seminar at Gottleib Duttweiler Institute in Zürich.

Gáspár-Ruppert W. (1991) *Die Spaß-Maschine. Der Computer im Alltag österreichischer Schüler/innen.* Vienna.

Gergely S. (1986) *Wie der Computer den Menschen und das Leben verändert.* Ein kritischer Ratgeber für Eltern, Lehrer und Schüler, München-Zürich: Piper Verlag.

Gumbo S. D. (1989) Training teachers and trainers. In UNESCO (1989) pp. 319-22.

Haefner K. (1980) The concept of an integrated system for information access and telecommunications (ISIT) and its impact on education in the 80s. In: S.H. Levington (ed.) *Information Processing 80.* North-Holland, Amsterdam.

Haefner K. (1981) Challenge of information technology to education: the new educational crisis. In: R. Lewis & D. Tagg (eds) *Computers in Education.* North-Holland, Amsterdam, pp. 525-31.

Harrison C. (ed.) (1987) *Interactive learning on the new technologies.* Report from the Educational research Workshop, Eindhoven, 2-5 June 1987. Swets Zeitlinger B.V. Amsterdam.

Hebenstreit J. (1988) Computers and Education: an encounter of the third kind. In: F. Lovis & D. Tagg (eds) *Proceedings of the 8th European Conference on Computers in education.* North-Holland, Elsevier Science Publishers B.V. Amsterdam pp. 3-11.

Jensen J.A. & Nissen T. (1987) On cognitive processes in education: a model for used knowledge based systyems in education. In: B. Sendov & S. Stanchev (1987) pp. 135-50.

Lauterbach R. (1987) New meanings in literacy. In Sendov & Stanchev (1987) pp. 83-101.

Legat H. (1988) *Computer im Unterricht.* Graz: Leykam Verlag.

Lehner K. & Reiter A. (1991) *EDP/Informatics in Austrian Education.* Federal Ministry of Education and the Arts, Vienna.

McDougall A. & Dowling C. (eds) (1990) *Computers in Education.* North Holland, Elsevier Science Publishers B.V. Amsterdam.

Mitzlaff H. & Wiederholt K. A. (eds) (1990) *Computer im Grundschulunterricht: Möglichkeiten und pädagogische Perspektiven.* McGraw-Hill, Hamburg .

OECD/CERI (1986) *New information technologies: a challenge for education.* OECD/CERI, Paris.

OECD/CERI (1987) *The introduction of computers in schools: the Norwegian experience.* Examiner's Report, OECD, Paris.

OECD (1988) *New technologies in the 1990s: a socio-economic strategy.* OECD, Paris.

Olson J. (1988) *Schoolworlds - Microworlds: computers and the culture of the classroom.* Pergamon Press.

Papert S. (1987) A critique of technocentrism in thinking about the school of the future. In: Sendov & Stanchev (1987) pp. 3-28.

Reiter A. & Rieder A. (eds) (1990) *Didaktik der Informatik: informations und kommunikationstechnische Grundbildung*, Wien: Jugend und Volk.

Sanders J. (1990) Computer equity of girls: what keeps it from happening? In: McDougall & Dowling (1990) pp. 181-7.

Schmidt E. (1990) Reality is an unending fairy tale. In: McDougall & Dowling (1990) pp. 617-22.

Sendov B. & Stanchev S. (eds) (1987) *Children in the Information Age.* Pergamon Press.

Schultz-Zander R. (1990) Concepts and strategies concerning informatics technology education for girls and young women. In: McDougall & Dowling (1990) pp. 195-200.

Taylor H. G. & Aiken K. M. (1991) *Informatics in secondary school.* Preprint of IFIP WG 3.1 Working Conference, The impacts of informatics on the organisation of education, University of California, Santa Barbara, USA, August 1991.

Turkle S. (1984) *The second self: computers and the human spirit.* New York.

UNESCO (ed) (1989) *Education and Informatics.* UNESCO, Paris.

van Weert T. (1987) Literacy in the information age. In: Sendov & Stanchev (1987) pp. 109-22.

van Weert T. (1991) *Informatics and the organisation of education.* Preprint of IFIP WG 3.1 Working Conference, The impacts of informatics on the organisation of education, University of California, Santa Barbara, USA, August 1991.

Winship J. A. (1989) *Information technologies in education: the quest for quality software.* OECD/SERI Report, Paris.

Vitalari N. P. (1990) Information technology in daily life: an assessment of the full integration hypothesis. In: J. Berleur, A. Clement, R. Sizer & D. Whitehouse (eds) *Information Society: evolving landscapes.* Springer-Verlag, New York, pp. 96-112.

Weizenbaum J. (1989) Keynote speech. Proceedings UNESCO Congress: *Education and Informatics: strengthening international co-operation.* 12-21 April 1989, Paris.

6

Karamjit S Gill, Tania Funston, Jim Thorpe,
Masao Hijitaka, John Gøtze

Individuals, culture and the design of information systems

6.1 Introduction

The following five pieces are reflections by members of the SEAKE Centre on what we feel are central issues about the relation of IT to social citizenship. We have not tried to impose or to arrive at a unity of viewpoint. We wrote separately but in consultation with one another.

6.2 The human-centred tradition

Karamjit S. Gill

Human centredness is a new technological tradition which places human need, skill, creativity and potentiality at the centre of the activities of technological systems. It is an emancipatory tradition which is rooted in the diversity of the cultural, scientific, and philosophical traditions of Europe. It is important to emphasise that it is not anti-technology or anti-science but a tradition which transcends the narrow mechanistic notions of science and technology (e.g. statistical control, objectivity, quantification), and crosses the boundaries of academic and working life disciplines. The tradition originated in Britain in the 1970s as an alternative to the Taylorist approach to production and the industrial rationalisation due to rapid advances in microelectronics. Since the 1970s it has influenced the development of culturally-oriented traditions in Europe, for example the "Humanisation of Technology" in Germany, and the "Democracy in Participation" in Scandinavia. These developments are now providing the creation of a new European tradition of "Anthropocentric Systems" which extends the industrial and manufacturing contexts of the human centred approaches to cultural contexts.

The rapid development of microelectronics in the 1970s gave rise to a wave of rationalisation in British industry. Workers at Lucas Aerospace put forward an action plan, the "Lucas Workers Plan", for socially useful products. The idea of human centredness was identified with production that was compatible with social needs and was determined by "use value" rather than just "exchange value", and in which workers have a right to play a dual role, as producers and consumers. Highly skilled engineers, technicians and skilled workers, who lost their jobs due to rationalisation, turned their protest into constructive ideas for socially useful products, and demonstrated in a practical and direct way the creative power of their own skills and abilities. The Plan "represented an enormous extension of consciousness" of "ordinary people" (Cooley, 1987).

Since the 1970s, the Lucas Plan has influenced the development of human centred approaches in other European nations, for example the concept of "Tool Perspective" and "Democracy in Participation" in Scandinavia, e.g. UTOPIA project (Ehn, 1988), and the "Humanisation of Technology and Work" (Dankbaar, 1987), and very recently "The Shaping of Technology and Work" in Germany (Corbett, 1990). These developments in human centredness in Europe are now contributing to the creation of a new European tradition of "Anthropocentric Systems" (Gill, 1990). At the heart of the new anthropocentric tradition lies the concept of diversity both in the philosophical sense and the cultural sense. Within the context of the European Community, it should be both democratic and rooted in culture, reflecting cultural and linguistic diversities. Although human centredness is essentially a European tradition, and may not map directly onto other cultures and nations, basic ideas of diversity, culture and industrial renaissance, anticipatory democracy, and holistic systems could provide a common basis for culturally-based human-centred traditions. Both the theory and practice of human-centred tradition are still open and are undergoing development. The attempt to maintain a mutually nutritious interplay between theoretical reflection and practical developments are central to the tradition.

6.3 IT and user involvement

Tania Funston

As recognition grows within the IT community of the development of software as a social process, the notion of *user involvement* has passed into the vocabulary of systems design, primarily as a means of integrating the intentions of the designer with the needs of the user. User involvement, however, is a term with many meanings, and does not of itself imply a participative process, if by participation we mean full entry to the decision-making process. It does not necessarily erode the designer's need to fit user requirements around the constraints of the system. Nor does it attempt to address wider issues of system design, within societal and qualitative perspectives. Indeed, it may imply the reverse, as there may only be a widening of the interest group, and further embedding of the perspectives of that group.

Technology, at a societal level, can be seen to be developed within existing power structures, both reflecting and consolidating the interests of the dominant social groupings within those structures. This operates at both political and ideological levels. Edwards (1990) for example, argues that computer work in the USA is "more than a job ...it is a major cultural practice, a large-scale social form that has created and reinforced modes of thinking, systems of interaction, and ideologies of social control" and goes on to relate this to a deeply embedded militaristic and masculine culture,which requires a hi-tech society to sustain it. Proponents of alternative approaches to technology , that is to the development of technologies which are non-alienating, non-exploitative and in harmony with our natural surroundings, have argued that in order to understand the nature of technology, it must be related to the patterns of production, consumption and general social activity that maintain the interests of the politically dominant section of the society in which it is developed. The social relations of production become reflected in the means of production.. technology and social patterns reinforce each other both materially and ideologically. (Dickson,1974; Pacey,1983) Feminist, ecological and human-centred thinking have contributed to the post-Kuhnian debate on preconceptions of technology. Science cannot be deemed the discovery of objective truth, nor can technology be considered to be an independent factor. Instead, it is the beliefs, or dominant ideologies, at work in different societies at different times which actually determine what is discovered, how it is discovered, and how it is interpreted and developed (Kuhn,1962; Keller,1985; Shiva,1989; Capra, 1982; Gill, 1986).

This debate suggests the emergence of a new epistemological paradigm, fuelled by the need to find new ways of understanding and dealing with the phenomenon of information technology and its rapid expansion, with the advent of the microcomputer, into all aspects of our lives. Inasmuch as technology can be seen to be shaped by the society which produces it, rather than as the practical outcome of objective scientific discovery, then its direction and application is not predetermined. It can be moulded, not only within power or profit motives, but in accordance with alternative and equally powerful beliefs, principles and values; those of democracy, equity, social justice and equality.

User-involved design, to use a generic term where none exists, can be viewed from this perspective. In any of its manifestations, it already represents a move away from an engineering perspective, dominant within system development practice, in which the central task is to deliver a product which can be formally specified and evaluated, often independent of the context in which it is placed. It is therefore a qualitative change of emphasis, although the shift may have a variety of motivations; the need to produce more effective systems by working more closely with users, the desire to increase job satisfaction, acknowledgement that the introduction of IT has far-reaching social and organisational implications, and at a profound level, the recognition that full user participation in design is an urgent necessity as the linear drive of technology becomes embedded in working life practices, subordinating the worker to the demands of the machine-centred system (Cooley, 1991). Good design, good design practice and good products which enhance human living requires the active contributions of *all* citizens. The task is too large to be left within the technical area alone. This in turn requires that all citizens feel *able* to contribute, an issue upon which all others rest. It also begs the question of what form contribution might take.

Within organisations the user involvement process is currently linked closely to particular hierarchical systems and corresponding delegation of decision-making power within organisations. Difficulties within this framework at a structural level are already recognised, as the consultation process may exclude those who actually use the systems, for example, the supermarket check-out operator whose direct experience both of the system-in-use and customer reaction may be unexamined and overlooked.

Meanwhile, for the ordinary citizen, for the remote end-user, the consumer, outside the sphere of action, far from the controversy of user-involved design,the possibility of participating in decision-making, or of any kind of reshaping of technology may seem remote or even unthinkable. In a world of rapid technological change, there may be an overwhelming sense of powerlessness to influence direction. We cannot avoid the impact of the computer, as we shop, visit the bank, or rather "the hole in the wall", pay our bills, or even catch a bus. This is a simple fact, but it is a most powerful element. The sense of technology as determined is reinforced by the volume of research on the impact and effects of technology. There is already a sense of acceptance, even in such a new situation, of a world planned and designed by others.

However, as information and communication technologies expand into every area of work and leisure, so the citizen becomes at one time end-user, a shop assistant checking transactions through an EPOS; at another time consumer, simply by making a telephone call through a network developed with the latest technology. Viewed in this way, fixed roles begin to break down. The individual moves not only through different roles in society, but also through varying life roles, sometimes passively, sometimes with authority. The all-powerful father may be the unnoticed employee. This lack of integration between public and private life may weaken the ability of the individual to assert himself or to feel he has anything to contribute. A classic example of this is the stay-at-home mother, once invisible, now encouraged to see herself as an experienced manager in a different setting. Nothing has changed here except the *perception* of the identity, but it is through changed perception that we can begin to effect changes in ourselves, and in our lives.

This is empowerment, in its only meaningful sense, the recognition of the power within oneself. The consumer has power, even it is only the power to accept or reject. This has been taken up in particular by the women's environmental movement in Japan, which places female purchasing power at the centre of their strategy for change. The end-user, the little person at the end of the process of technological innovation, has the power of indifference or accidental sabotage, in fact a most daunting power. In any organisational setting, irrespective of technology, what can be more threatening to enthusiasts of co-operative, across the board teamworking than the person who finds the process boring or irrelevant?

Yet these are not seen as active roles, although group process theory (Tajfel, 1979) provides insights into individual and group reactions to issues of power and control. Our view of power is so influenced by systems of categorisation, by the pecking order - women and blacks last but for Equal Opportunities- that we judge our own effectiveness in terms of the position we occupy in society, rather than by our effectiveness as human beings, each with a contribution to make. In particular we have to break the barrier of separateness. Our working lives are separate from our private lives, ourselves from others, men from women, our beliefs from our practices, our use from our involvement, our position as members of an advanced technological society from our notion of ourselves as technologically literate.

This is most clearly seen in the case of women, who are the users of modern technologies, both at home and in the workplace, yet often see themselves as apart from, and ignorant of technology. The perception is stronger than the reality, and leads to a surrendering of involvement. Yet the perception is created not just by the individual, but by the society which espouses such thinking , and by the structures within which work is carried out. Women may by conditioning not see themselves as computer-literate, or structurally in a position to comment on their experiences as workers. Where is the sense of participation, of excitement in developing new tools and new ways of working? The gap between design and use is at its widest here.

At the most profound level change must begin with perception, a knowledge which informed the creation of awareness and consciousness-raising groups in an earlier era, focusing not on action, but on process. Adding to these teachings of psychoanalytical theory is the development of experiential therapies, reuniting mind and body, the rational and the emotional, in a reflection of new holistic thinking in our society.

These kind of insights help us to recognise and to value the existence of different kinds of knowledge, and to understand the ways in which, for example, our society privileges the rational over the intuitive and rationally divides the organisation of society into discrete categories, health, education, the law, etc., to the extent that interrelated and interdependent issues such as poverty and health cannot easily be dealt with. Our capabilities are diminished by fragmentation. In the same way we isolate the practice of design from use practice, thus preventing any kind of dynamic interaction between the two. As we begin to see the separations which are characteristic of our society we can begin to make linkages between this and our view of ourselves as individuals, in some way separate from and unrelated to societal forces, and therefore powerless, excluded from decision-making. It is from this perspective that we can begin to affect structural change, and not the reverse.

However, we cannot move easily from where we are to a qualitatively different position. The constraints are both psychological and structural. It is comfortable to remain with ingrained habits of thinking, especially within structures which support them. Studies of innovation show us that new ideas and ways are taken up by a few, and only gradually become common belief, in a process which is probably a testing for validity. What then are the circumstances and where are the frameworks within which awareness can develop, perception change and a sense of empowerment take root and grow?

Firstly, there must be motivation - a perceived need for change, or perhaps only a feeling of discomfort and discontent. Secondly, there must be involvement. This requires a role. Engagement cannot take place in a vacuum. Thirdly, there must be an environment which supports and facilitates learning. Awareness grows through learning, if it is learning through direct engagement, through learning-by-doing, through exploration, through tentatively and then more boldly exercising judgment. This kind of learning process can only take place within organisations under certain circumstances - when people feel that they are free to bring all of themselves to the situation, their knowledge and their feelings, that they are able to directly apply their experiences and to express both positive and negative feelings about processes and outcomes, and that their views have some significance, that they are listened to. Learning will be closed off unless the group can feel really in control, that is, not subject to managerial dictate or unannounced policy change. This is a very threatening situation for management, but if such an approach can be shown to be beneficial to the organisation, then it may be accepted.

In a different context, Turkle (1990) shows how creativity in using the computer can be repressed when its power as an expressive medium is denied and educational computing remains blind to the need to work through problems in an authentic personal style. The penalties are high - talent is wasted, self-image eroded, people drop out and the contributions of those who stay in are limited.

These are conditions which apply to those who are brought into a consultation process. What of those who are not? Even within organisations, the problem of the end-user keeps recurring. In the last analysis, emphasis within systems design is on product. The issue of what involvement means reproduces itself when the design cycle ends, and the product in use passes inevitably into a different set of hands. Hales (1991) points out the limits of cooperative design in one example in which excellent practice neither resulted in learning for the whole organisation, nor addressed organisational and job design issues. Design and use are separate stages. Participation in design does not guarantee satisfaction in use?

What then is the framework which allows us to break out of these closed circles? We have to begin to take the notion of user involvement beyond the perspective of *design* into that of *evaluation*. Through this we can conceptually extend the cycle of design, implementation and use to include the end-user. In widening our concept of what the purpose of user involvement is, that is,to open up the whole area of technological development to the scrutiny of all, we at once widen our perspective and create space for the unexpected, the unpredictable, and the dynamic, precisely those ingredients which are missing in closed systems. At the same time our notion of participative working needs to be extended beyond an emphasis on what takes place in the closed group. It is not just active doing which is valuable; reflection has its place too. Evaluation, as considered here, is not a formal process, which reaches a conclusion (albeit one which can be repeated). Rather it is a continuous, never-ending process, a continual reflection on how things are. The contribution of the end-user can be precisely this, a commentary on experience itself, the kind of acquired knowledge which is considered too subjective and personal to be useful in design. This will not be found unless it is sought, unless it is considered to be necessary.

One example: a conversation with a sales rep. Within minutes he has described not just his reactions to using a computerised system in his working life but an account of the ways in which the new style of working fails to take into account the local situation (distance versus time needed to enter no go areas in Northern Ireland, doing business slowly over a cup of tea); the ergonomic aspects (the laptop does not fit on his knee in the driving seat, his usual position for writing up his reports), the implications for family life (he cannot pick up his son from school and then go back to work, as his working hours are now monitored); his relationship with his customers, whom he no longer visits at their convenience in the evening, as it takes him much longer to input details of the day's sales. He goes on to outline how the present system could be adjusted. There is simply no mechanism for feeding back this kind of information, nor for taking up the suggestions which arise from it. Nor would the salesman volunteer it. " They're not interested in what I think."

If we can conceive of involvement as continual feedback at different levels, in design, implementation, use and evaluation, at both micro and macro level, we can begin to envisage a larger and more holistic picture of interaction and participation, an interplay between those who develop technology and those who use it. If we can take up the notion of technology as socially shaped, continually evolving, then the emphasis shifts to process. The outcome of systems development is not only a product, but also a process of mutual learning, not just about the tools but about the environment in which the tools are placed, and their appropriateness, and how they could be improved or relocated or abandoned. At the moment these options are not open to us because the cycle of development is contained, and not by definition responsive to or linked with a wider environment.

Educators have a role to play in this. How many university courses in Britain encourage students to consider technology as theirs to develop? How many look at information technology in society? How many training courses go beyond the instilling of technical competence? How many courses designed to attract women into careers in science and technology focus on access rather than the causes and thus perhaps the remedies for alienation? How often are people encouraged to be creative in their approaches to technology? Facilitating raised awareness of these issues can turn passivity into positive action.

User involvement will not imply more than a refinement of an existing decision-making process if there is no opening up to the wider environment, no engagement with the underlying drives in our society, and no opportunity for reflection, on who we are and where we stand. It is not however a sudden leap forward. Change can only begin from where we are. We can only change our realities by starting with our perceptions. From this point we can begin to see how they could be different.

6.4 Tensions local and global

Jim Thorpe

To choose *Social Citizenship* as a title for a conference seems to mark the uncertainties about the relative stress that should be placed upon the social and on the individual in the design of our future in such spheres as education, industry and the environment. The currency of self-contradictory slogans such as "Social Citizenship" signals a society on the move from one world view to the next; and there are problems because we are crossing the boundary between one stable form of existence and another. The slogan signals the new emphasis on the social whilst acknowledging the hitherto prevailing individualism implicit in the notion of citizen. The distinction between the social and the individual is mirrored by the dilemma between how far the future is to be planned and how far it simply emerges from the activities and intentions of individuals and groups. The remarks in this piece attempt neither completeness nor a linear argument, but are an exploration of the notion that tension between polar opposites lies at the heart of dynamically stable social systems.

If we are to rely on the activity of planning, i.e. designing the future, how do we ensure the relevance of our plans to the life and work of the people who will be affected by the outcome of the planning? Is it enough to rely on the expertise of existing planners, or do we have work in a new way in each project? There are established skills and experience based upon professional practice that designers may draw upon to make their work efficient; but is the outcome necessarily of relevance to those who use the designed artifacts or live in the designed environment? If not we may have to consider participatory planning.

The conflict between efficiency and relevance, or effectiveness of decision-making procedures, is one that is echoed elsewhere. For example, in the design of assessment procedures, between the requirements of *validity* or relevance on the one hand, and *reliability*, on the other. (Assessment is about decision making. Indeed, assessment is but a ritual when it is not designed to answer a question.) The most relevant form of assessment of competence of an activity is one which is based upon performance of the activity itself. This view is used to argue for assessing student performance by profiles and by continuous assessment rather than subjecting them to special assessment tasks. The counter argument is that a formal procedure, based upon the same assessment tasks faced by all students is less dependent on local circumstances of the test situation.

People are differently inclined about whether they stress validity or stress reliability. The two requirements are in conflict, reflecting the opposing characteristics of fitting to the individual circumstances and standardisation. Such conflicts between requirements were in evidence in the manufacture of rifles, an early example of industrial automation in the USA. Crafted construction, i.e. individual fitting, leads to better guns but to non-interchangeability of parts, as well as less efficient production.

Decisions are often thought of as being about clear situations where they may be taken automatically by procedure, for example stock re-ordering when quantities fall below given levels, or about fuzzy situations when human judgment is essential. Computerised decision making may replace human judgment in routine applications but not where information is incomplete or evaluation of possible outcomes uncertain, because the decisions depend upon idiosyncratic preference or alternative interests which would be served by a different range of outcomes. The centrality of diverse perspectives and interests is what makes decision-making essentially problematic.

Arguments for participation in the development of the future or in the design of artifacts are about *relevance* of the products of design. In this respect I see arguments for participation couched in terms of democratic ideals as being about relevance. Counter-arguments concern the need for efficiency in the planning process and the impossibility of obtaining adequate participation. We may hear the question, "How can we expect participants to have the range of analytical and communication skills necessary to participate?"

I believe there are deep issues to be faced about the ability to participate. Arguments about *ability* are sometimes referred to in terms of literacy problems. At the time of writing, the British Government is making a play for the need for "basic skills" as a citizen's right. We also hear about the need for "computer literacy". It seems easier to talk about needs if we can refer to them as procedures which can be taught - or at least that can be assessed. We may say that understanding is a goal, but we can only test behaviour. I believe that we need to consider literacy - or literacies - as more than merely simply performance skills. We need to see literacies as being about *social practice*, as Tacchi puts it, that is as means by which we encounter and place ourselves in the world. We do so in more-or-less common and in more-or-less idiosyncratic ways. If literacy is too tightly defined then we are all made dyslexic in one way or another by our incapacity to cope fully with all the formal media in prescribed ways. If on the other hand we are able to negotiate the media, the discourse, we employ, then participation by the many becomes more possible.

I have attempted to explore what I see as the inevitable conflict between specialist skill and application in local situations when human judgment can be employed, and the global situation where standard procedures replace the judgment which can no longer be exercised because individuals do not have sufficient overall knowledge and where a variety of interests have to be reflected in decision making.

6.5 A crossroad of IT and culture

Masao Hijikata

There is a difficulty in applying IT to unfamiliar situations which arises because the theory of IT exists, necessarily, at a general level, so that deciding what is appropriate in a particular cultural context is not automatic. If we are to think about how to apply IT we need to understand the culture in which the IT systems are to be implemented. I will examine the notions of the (meta-)discipline of IT and of culture as a basis for considering the relation between them. The IT discipline I see as an *abstract* discipline, whereas I want to consider *culture* from a concrete perspective - that is, in terms of objects, artifacts, and patterns of behaviour existing within what I shall term a "cultural unit". What follows is a series of remarks rather than anything like an exhaustive examination.

We often use the term "culture" to underpin our descriptions of social situations or processes. But this term is too vague, coming from too general a level to allow us to understand problems within society. Here I would like to use the term "culture" in a rough fashion to refer to *primitive knowledge patterns* which generate the behaviour which constitutes human daily life. This means that even if the political or institutional system varies, there is a stable knowledge pattern which we may call the "cultural pattern". Of course the "cultural pattern" has to change in order to adapt to environmental change, but in a time scale of hundreds of years. However, as planners, we are only able to deal with problems occurring ten years into the future. So, from this perspective cultural patterns are stable.

When we stand at the crossroads of modern information technology and culture, we immediately encounter problems. Modern information technology developed as a meta-science because information and knowledge are essential *general* factors that shape a culture everywhere and in every era. Universality is thus the central characteristic of information science and technology as it develops increasingly general or abstract theories to allow it to encompass an ever widening diversity of IT artifacts. This increasing generality means that information theory alone is insufficient to deal with any practical problems. When we try to apply these fruitful ideas developed by modern information science and technology to cultural issues, serious problems arise as a consequence of the remoteness of the meta-science of IT from the practical problems that it helps to solve, in contrast to theories associated with earlier technologies which are more organically related to them.

We learn from the history of science that science and technology emerged from a specialised cultural background - for example traditional machinery technology was developed in the process of British industrialisation and had world-wide influence because each culture wanted to attain economic growth and to shape a competitive edge. I do not intend to explain the relation between traditional scientific development and world-wide competitiveness, but I do intend to compare traditional science and information technology. On the surface, traditional technological development which has clear objectives that enable human physical power to be extended seems to be transferred from one culture to another culture smoothly although submerged cultural problems do occur.

The position of information technology is, however, quite different. The theory of information technology can never suggest anything about social value by itself because it is a meta-science. When we look for a basis on which to develop information technology, we have to confess that the design of information systems (including how to apply information technology to social affairs), and the design of the social affairs themselves are totally independent issues. This is because the design of information systems is an activity which converges to specific functionality, whereas the design of social affairs employs the functionality to serve divergent human values. We have to develop a conception of design which allows mediation between the two kinds of design.

Design of social affairs belongs to the domain of cultural problems. When we think about the cultural problems related to human values in general, especially in the concrete situation, at first we have to identify the *cultural unit* because cultural issues may be viewed in terms of a set of conditions, including historical background and physical circumstances. Divergence in cultural affairs based on individualism will be coalesced in the cultural unit. Then how may we identify the unit? The answer will depend on the problem situation such as the different traditions of the East and West in the context of scientific traditions, or national level or regional level in the context of economical issues, or organisation in the context of industrial culture. Each unit has its own cultural infrastructures which represent the adaptation that has taken place over time of each unit to its corresponding environment.

When we not only analyse but also intend to solve the problem by seeing it as a design problem, it is not the universal but the local knowledge which is dominant in the concrete cultural problem situation, although we may start from an abstract view. Universal knowledge can only *stimulate* local knowledge, it can never be applied directly. Local knowledge should be dominant in the concrete stage because local knowledge has stood the test of time in its application to local problems.

Information has destroyed many boundaries - for example the boundaries of traditional academic fields, or the borders of countries, etc. If we only examine concepts of information from such a general viewpoint in our attempt to discover the functions of information, we end up floating in a muddy sea of information flow, and then the "information society" begins to walk by itself as a creation of our talk and our society will be fragile, bereft of practical designs.

Now we stand at the crossroads. One way is named "information circulation road". On this road, *knowledge transfer* which comes from the idea of *knowledge circulation* is the dominant problem. And this road seems smoggy. The other way is "information stock road". Experimental knowledge which belongs to the tacit dimension of knowledge is the dominant problem here. And this road seems smoggy, too.

We must seriously pay attention to design problems concerned with constructing the junction of IT and culture. I suppose participatory design methodology is a central methodology in order to design the junction. And nowadays, new perspectives of design which connect two roads are urgently needed. I am deeply interested in the issues of an up-dated concept of social citizenship in the context of participatory design of regional planning because it will be a basic idea to the issues related to divergence and convergence in design.

In Japan, the central aspect of regional planning is moving from economical development to quality of life, including environmental problems in these days. It means that an interdisciplinary and participatory approach to the cultural issues is essential in the planning process. Information environment becomes richer than before in social life, however it is more difficult for the local authorities to make an integrated plan because of the diversity of opinions and increasing uncertainty. A new methodology which enables, on one hand, to manage the information which should be applied in the planning process, and, on the other hand, to be a bridge between the past and the future, seems to me virtually necessary.

6.6 From user friendly systems to human-centred design

John Gøtze

In the past decade or so, there has been a trend among system designers towards designing more "user friendly" and "easy-to-learn" systems. One idea is *graphic interfaces*, where icons, symbols and pictures are used to make the systems easier to grasp and to handle - "a picture is worth a thousand words". Another idea is *natural language interfaces*, where normal real-world language and symbols are used instead of the abstract and procedural language of computers.

The latest addition to this trend is adaptive (or learning) systems, which have the ability to adapt automatically to the altering behaviour of the user; such systems usually work on the basis of an internal AI model of the user, which has been generated by an observation, classification and storage of the user's behaviour in different situations (Friedrich, 1990).

Initiatives such as these are at a first glance laudable, and might even facilitate beneficial computer usage in alternative domains of non-professionals such as school children, elderly people, handicapped, etc. Also, the initiatives put some real concerns on the agenda - the problem of acceptability of complex systems versus user qualifications and training. There are, however, some emerging problems in following this approach. The main critique against this approach of adaptivity aims at the fact that the user is condemned to passivity and strongly reduced with respect to his chance to learn (ibid.). The user is "driving", not "commanding" (Winograd & Flores, 1986).

Adaptive, "user-friendly" systems, - including much AI research - could therefore be looked upon as an attempt to find technical functional solutions to problems which have arisen in the social practice, i.e. the user interaction with computers. That the limitations of people are counterbalanced by the powerful new information technologies, is the point of view. However, the subjectivity of the user, or others affected by the systems, becomes invisible for the design process, and, indeed, the designer. The socially constructed nature of reality is obscured and is replaced by measurable and computable objectivities. Thus reality, at the end of the day, is exhaustible. But, reality is not exhaustible, in fact it is inexhaustible.

The contingencies faced in any human action inevitably overthrow the very best plans and designs. As pointed out by Suchman (1987), "the relation of the intent to accomplish some goal to the actual course of situated action is enormously contingent". Plans may of course be conceived by actors prior to action but they are not simply executed in the actions. Action is infinitely rich compared to the plan and cannot be exhausted by a plan (Schmidt, 1991).

Our approach, which we call human-centred, is an attempt to establish an alternative design methodology which caters for the above mentioned issues. The aim is to create a methodology of and practice in design that has as a starting point the *use situation*, and looks upon computer systems as support systems, i.e. as useful tools which enable people to perform tasks they might not have been able to otherwise carry out effectively. Instead of emphasising the potential of the technology itself and stressing the limitations of people, the human centred approach seeks to develop the creative and productive capabilities of human beings to a far greater extent through work with machines. Rosenbrock (1977) encapsulates the idea of human centredness as "to use the best technology that we know, but to make it an aid to those who work with it, so that their work becomes an enrichment, not an impoverishment of their humanity, and so that the resource which their abilities represent is used to the highest degree"

References

Capra, F. (1982) *The turning point.* Fontana, London.

Cooley, M. (1987) *Architect or Bee?: the human price of technology.* Hogarth Press, London.

Cooley, M. (1991) *Architect or bee? the human price of technology.* (2nd ed.) Hogarth Press, London.

Corbett, J.M. (1990) *Crossing the border.* Springer-Verlag, New York.

Dankbaar, B. (1987) Social assessment of workplace technology - some experiences with the German programme "Humanization of Work" *Research Policy,* **16**, pp.337-52.

Dickson, D. (1974) *Alternative technology and the politics of technical change.* Fontana, London.

Edwards, P. N. (1990) The army and the micro-world. Computers and the politics of gender identity. *Signs: Journal of Women in Culture and Society* **16**,1.

Ehn, P. (1988) *Work oriented design of computer artifacts.* Swedish Centre for Working Life, Stockholm.

Friedrich, J. (1990) Industrial Cultural Influences on the Development of Information Technology. Paper presented at the *International Workshop on Industrial Culture and Human Centred Systems,* May 14-18th 1990, Tokyo Keizai University.

Gill, K.(ed.) (1986) *Artificial intelligence for society.* John Wiley, Chichester.

Gill, K. (1990) *Summary of Human Centred Systems research in Europe.* SEAKE Centre, Brighton.

Hales, M. (1991) User participation in design - what it can deliver, what it can't and what this means for management. *Paper for SPRU/CICT workshop on policy issues in systems and software development.* Brighton, UK.

Keller, E. F. (1985) *Reflections on gender and science.* Yale University Press, Yale.

Kuhn, T.S.(1962) *The structure of scientific revolutions.* University of Chicago Press, Chicago.

Pacey, A. (1983) *The culture of technology.* Blackwell, Oxford.

Rosenbrock, H. H. (1977) The Future of Control. *Automatica,* **13.**

Schmidt, K. (1991) Riding a Tiger, or Computer Supported Cooperative Work. *Proceedings of European conference on CSCW '91.* Amsterdam, The Netherlands.

Shiva, V.(1989) *Staying alive- women, ecology and development.* Zed Books, London.

Suchman, L. (1987) *Plans and Situated Actions - The problem of human-machine communication.* Cambridge University Press, Cambridge.

Tacchi, J. (1991) *Literacy and the Social Self,* unpublished MA dissertation, Sussex University.

Tajfel, H.(1979) Individuals and groups in social psychology. *British Journal of Social and Clinical Psychology,* **18**, 183-190.

Turkle, S.(1990) Style as substance in educational computing. In: Berleur,J. et al (eds.) *The information society:evolving landscapes.* Springer-Verlag, New York.

Winograd, T. & Flores, F. (1986) *Understanding Computers and Cognition. A New Foundation for Design.* Ablex Publishing Corporation, N.J.

7

Simone Fischer-Hübner & Morton Swimmer

Social aspects of computer viruses

7.1 Introduction

Computer viruses[1] are no longer exclusively in the domain of universities. There has been an alarming increase of cases in the public and private sector. Soon nearly every personal computer (PC) user will have come into contact with a virus at least once. Meanwhile, the number of different viruses for the IBM-PCs and compatibles is rising daily. Presently, there are approximately 1500 viruses, whereas in 1988 we counted only twelve! Viruses have been written for many different systems, including mainframes. Just as the awareness of the lack of computer security and persistence is changing the way we view information technology, viruses are having a negative influence on working life.

In this paper, we discuss the technical reasons for the lack of viral protection, give examples of the impact of viruses on people's work and private lives, speculate on who is programming the viruses and what legal and ethical issues are involved.

7.2 Technical misconceptions

7.2.1 Terminology

For the rest of the paper the terms "virus", "Trojan horse", and "worm" will occur frequently. There is still much confusion over the exact definitions of the various computer anomalies, even amongst computer specialists. This has led to many misunderstandings. To this day there are no generally accepted definitions of all types of malicious software, but the following definitions have been used in recent years in the Virus Test Center:

Definition 1

A *computer virus* is a non-autonomous set of routines that can modify programs or systems so that they contain executable copies of itself. A virus may also

---

[1] For simplicity, we will refer to computer viruses as viruses for the rest of the paper, unless a misunderstanding is possible.

contain a routine that performs a function unrelated to the actual viral property, such as a screen effect or the destruction of data.

Definition 2
A *Trojan horse* is an autonomous program that masquerades as a harmless function but, unknown to the user, contains a hidden function that can be destructive.

Definition 3
A *worm* is a set of programs or routines that can independently, or with the help of an unsuspecting user, propagate throughout a network of autonomous computers.

Our definitions of viruses and worms are variations of the mathematical definition of the term computer virus (Cohen, 1986). Unfortunately, the mathematical definition also includes such legitimate MS-DOS programs as DISKCOPY. We have taken the more pragmatic view that stresses the technical differences between worms and viruses.

7.2.2 Why today's systems cannot guarantee security and fight the virus threat

During recent years, the number of software anomalies has grown exponentially and other serious threats, such as intrusion by hackers, are constantly demonstrating the vulnerability of present-day systems. Unfortunately, IT-security is based on some misconceptions. Terms such as "Secure System" or "Secure Operating System" are misleading as today's systems cannot guarantee security in its general meaning and especially cannot prevent the threat from computer viruses. In this section, some reasons for this problem will be explained.

Computer Security covers the three characteristics

- confidentiality (protection from unauthorised disclosure);
- integrity (guarantee that data contains the correct physical and semantic representation of information);
- availability (guarantee that resources are available).

Security criteria catalogues such as the American Orange Book (US Dept of Defense, 1985) and the European ITSEC (ITSEC, 1991) define different security classes for security measures that can be implemented. Unfortunately, they concentrate on confidentiality and neglect aspects of integrity and availability, although the latter are no less important in fighting vulnerability in commercial applications (see Brunnstein and Fischer-Hübner, 1990). The Orange Book primarily serves the interests of the military for data secrecy and exclusively covers increasing demands on system confidentiality in its hierarchically structured security classes. The European ITSEC was influenced by the ideas in the Orange Book and also by interests of the secret services. According to ITSEC security, functions may either be individually specified or they may be defined by reference to a predefined functionality-class. Besides the five hierarchically structured predefined example functionality classes for classifying confidentiality (that correspond to the functionality of the classes C1, C2, B1, B2, B3 of the Orange Book), they define only one class for classifying system integrity (F-IN) and just one class for classifying demands of system availability (F-AY).

The catalogues mirror the biased technical development of IT security. Having been funded primarily by the United States (US) government, most security endeavours have concentrated on secrecy of classified information. This tradition has persisted even in commercial applications, although their primary goal should have been integrity (Gasser, 1988, p. 4). Most security mechanisms in use are mechanisms to control the legality of the system usage to guarantee confidentially. Mainly mechanisms for identification and authentication, auditing and for discretionary and mandatory access control are used for the enforcement of confidentiality. Access controls, especially mandatory access controls, are often based on formal security models such as the Bell/LaPadula model (Bell and LaPadula, 1973). For enforcing integrity, the same or similar mechanisms are used. Integrity models such as the Biba model (Biba, 1977) or Clark/Wilson model (Clark and Wilson, 1987) also require access control mechanisms for their enforcements. The Clark/Wilson model enforces the principle of well formed transactions and separation of duty. Each access control list entry reconciles an object with a user and a program that accesses it and the rights associated with this action. Unfortunately, models and appropriate mechanisms for enforcing integrity are very seldomly used. Furthermore, it is arguable that we need other forms of models and mechanisms to enforce integrity that are not based solely on access rights, but also consider the semantics of stored data. Availability has not traditionally been a topic of security research either and for its enforcement other techniques are used.

According to the security criteria catalogues, systems with high security demands will be developed by using formal models and formal specification and verification methods. Formal security models usually define "security" as the fulfilment of certain security properties and show that by starting in a "secure" state and by applying the model's rules these security properties will be fulfilled, i.e. the system will remain in a secure state. The Bell/LaPadula model for example defines "security" as the fulfilment of the simple, the ≈ (star), and the discretionary security property. Formal specification and verification techniques are used to prove the correspondence of the system with the underlying formal security model.

Today's IT security, based on such concepts, obviously has its limitations. To guarantee "security" in its general meaning it has to be guaranteed that the system is generally not improperly used. The model's definitions of "security" often reduce the term "security" to only a few security properties. Consequently, even systems with the highest security ratings according to the criteria cannot be regarded as "secure" in its general meaning. These systems are also vulnerable to new kinds of attack strategies, that are unknown so far and have not been considered in the system design. Insider threats and threats that are spread over a longer period can hardly be detected. Furthermore, there are insecurity problems that are not decidable in general. Cohen has proved that the virus property is generally undecidable by transferring this problem to the halting problem of Turing machines. Consequently, such kinds of security threats cannot generally be prevented on even verified "secure" systems that implement security models. Cohen also practically demonstrated how a system that had the Bell/LaPadula and the Biba model implemented could still be infected by viruses.

Heuristic methods for intrusion detection that are based on the hypothesis that intrusions can be detected by observing the system usage for statistically abnormal behaviour, and are independent of any particular system vulnerability, could help but cannot guarantee security either. Heuristic expert system rules for virus detection could be defined that raise the probability of detection of known and new viruses (see Brunnstein, Fischer-Hübner and Swimmer, 1991).

Another reason viruses can hardly be prevented by today's systems is due to the lack of integrity considerations. Viruses are a threat to the integrity of a system. As mentioned before, integrity aspects have been neglected and effective integrity control mechanisms are missing. Access control lists that, besides the subject, also record the program that may be used to get a specific access to an object, may prevent a program illegally modifying another program. Wichers *et al.* propose a so called Program Access Control List (PACL) mechanism for virus protection (Wichers *et al.*, 1990). Unfortunately such mechanisms, also required by the Clark/Wilson model, are very rarely implemented. Consequently, although until now viruses have been mainly a threat to personal computers (PCs), malicious software cannot be prevented by systems that are supposed to be "secure" either.

Although PC software vendors often claim that they have developed antivirus software that can detect or even prevent all kind of viruses, such protection can never be reached. Only antivirus software such as scanners that can detect the infection of all known viruses, or programs that can detect changes caused by viruses (for example, by the use of checksumming techniques) or typical behaviour patterns of viruses, as well as organisational and recovery plans can help to cope with the virus threat.

7.3 The impact of computer viruses

There is no technical reason why viruses should not exist on all types of computers, including mainframes. However, the problem is greatest on the IBM-PCs and compatibles. Here we have over 1500 different viruses, and many are fairly sophisticated and destructive. There are practically no bounds as to what a virus may do, so long as it can be done by software[2] . Some of the earliest viruses were destructive. For instance, the Israeli virus deleted files on every Friday the 13th and the Vienna virus destroyed one out of every eight files infected. More recently viruses have become more clever in their destruction. The Dark Avenger virus overwrites random sectors on the disk, so that even the back-ups may prove worthless. Whereas there are still more non-destructive viruses, the tendency is definitely towards destructive viruses.

Even otherwise harmless viruses have proved themselves destructive due to side effects. The MS-DOS operating system is a completely open system. No portion of it is protected in memory or on disk. Many procedures, e.g. for going memory-resident, are not well defined and badly controlled. Furthermore, many viruses attempt to multi-task, something MS-DOS was not built for and does not support. This leads to many conflicts between the virus and other programs, including the operating system. The newer stealth viruses are often even more problematic. The results are difficult to estimate. They can range from programs not running any more, to the whole file system becoming garbled and thereby unusable.

7.3.1 Cases

To illuminate the impact that viruses can have, we have gathered a few cases that demonstrate the problems involved. The cases are not entirely fictional. Sometimes only the names have been changed, others are fictional but representative.

Case 1

It was a Friday the 13th in 1988. Mrs Meyer had been annoyed by her computer the entire week. It was getting noticeably slower and sometimes the screen did strange things: a small rectangle of text would shift. She had asked her colleague, who was her department's computer "freak" and often brought in computer games, about this, but was not taken seriously. When Mrs Meyer tried to start her word processor, it was not there! She then tried the spreadsheet - gone! Every program she tried was gone. Other colleagues were having the same problem and soon the whole department was in pandemonium. Most of the work had to be done manually and most workers had to stay late. On the next Monday a technician came but could not find the problem. He reinstalled all programs as the data was still there, and everything seemed OK, until the next Friday the 13th!

Case 2

Mr Roy bought himself a computer in Bergedorf, near Hamburg, for doing the bookkeeping for a theatre club. When installing an address program, it was

---

2 Contrary to rumours, it is very difficult to harm the hardware via software, although possible. No virus to date has attempted this.

noticed that every 5 minutes a melody would play, and it was not possible to use the PC while the melody was playing. When asked about this odd behaviour, it was said that this was a "feature" included right from the beginning. It turned out that the computer salesman had accidentally infected not only Mr Roy's but also other computers sold at the shop with the Oropax virus. Fortunately it was a non-destructive virus and only prevented the normal use of the PC while "in action". (The name Oropax comes from a brand of ear plugs.)

Case 3

Strange things were happening to Mrs Schmidt's computer. Whenever she started a new program, her PC would beep at her. Once this had happened, it never beeped again for that program. She notified a technician. He thought it must be a virus and immediately performed a low level format. Months of work was lost. It should be noted that the virus was, in fact, the Vaksina virus that is not destructive, and, besides beeping, has no other action.

In the beginning, when the subject of viruses was still young, instructing users about the dangers of computer viruses was difficult. Often the idea was not taken seriously. If the media took up the subject they often misrepresented the problems. Many myths were circulated and many have stuck until today. Because of the lack of knowledge, damage was done by either not taking action where action was needed or the action taken was out of proportion to the danger.

Case 4

Dipl. Ing. Wolf was finishing the layouts for a client. He had been working day and night to meet the deadline, leaving the computer on for the short spells of sleep he allowed himself. Just as he was doing some last minute changes to a drawing, a message flashed onto the screen: Warning!! Don't turn off the power or remove the diskette while Disk Killer is Processing ... PROCESSING ... Now you can turn off the power. I wish you luck.

He had heard of the Virus Test Center and contacted us. At the time it was thought that the damage this virus does was recoverable. He sent his entire hard disk up to Hamburg. A closer analysis of the virus and the hard disk revealed that it was nearly impossible to recover the data. Even though the author of the virus had included the means to recover the data, he had overlooked three major mistakes making data recovery impossible. Luckily for Mr. Wolf, he had back-ups that were only a week old.

There are reports of small businesses going bankrupt partially due to the effects of viruses. So many firms are increasingly dependent on computers and information processing that the loss of the computer services would bring the firm to a standstill, sometimes terminally. Larger firms are usually less vulnerable. They usually do their main work on mainframes, so that the PCs are expendable, but this is changing. There is a clear movement away from centralised processing and to local area networks based on microcomputers. Fortunately, many viruses often have problems running on networks, but the day may come when a virus will take down an entire bank!

Case 5

A medium-sized military contractor was hit with the Stoned virus. Despite the policy of no data media to be brought in or out of the firm, due to restrictive spending on software much software used was not acquired by the firm. The virus was found by an antivirus brought in by an employee. Although only one department was hit by the virus, the management ordered an inspection of all PCs for the virus and also for software that was being illegally used. Much of the control over the PCs was centralised and individual freedom in the use of PCs was curtailed.

Sadly, this seems to happen in many larger firms when struck by a virus. The computer departments jump at the opportunity to regain lost terrain by introducing security measures against viruses. Sometimes these measures are justified, but often enough they go too far. Privacy issues are completely ignored by periodic "searches" for games and pirated software. Personal or departmental interests are ignored by bureaucratising software acquisition. Apart from the effects on the work climate, the efficiency of the firm may also deteriorate. On the other hand, much positive work has been done in large corporations in dealing with the virus problem. At the Virus Test Center we have been dealing with the problems these firms have had since 1988 and, especially over the last year, we have received fewer calls from large corporations (until the beginning of 1992, when we received 28 sacks of inquiries about the Michelangelo virus, many from large firms). This is mainly due to measures taken by the staff, be it routinely scanning for viruses, restrictive use of the PC, or other antivirus software. In a particularly good case, a large pharmaceutical firm employed a specialist to assist the employees when security problems arise.

Case 6

One large German computer hardware retailer had serious problems with viruses. Besides having local problems in their shops, there was an incident where the Stoned virus was shipped with some hardware. Then, in the summer of 1991, the Michelangelo virus was shipped with a Super-VGA card. It should be noted that the perpetrator was not the retailer but the manufacturer in Taiwan, but the retailer failed to recognise the infection and was ultimately left with the problem. This time the retailer decided to acknowledge the problem and to offer a free antivirus with every PC sold.

This retailer was the first one in Germany to acknowledge the problem and offer a remedy free to the customer. In the USA, IBM did better. They started the High Integrity Computer Lab a few years ago to deal with computer security threats. They have a good antivirus which is available to all IBM distributors. Most retailers and wholesalers still try to play down the problem, as the firm Commodore did. We have been sent a letter by the firm asking us not to "disquiet their potential customers" [3].

7.3.2 Extent of damage

But how to quantify the damage inflicted on society by computer viruses? There have been some attempts to quantify the damage expressed in pecuniary terms. No attempts have been made to quantify user freedom, mistrust and other less tangible ideas. The most famous attempt to put a figure on virus damage was done by Tippett (Tippett, 1991). Tippett provided a mathematical model for the spread of viruses over the computer community. He also performed a survey to test his hypotheses. Tippett based his model on the assumptions that: (1) viruses run flawlessly, (2) the majority of computers has no inherent resistance to viruses, and (3) the replication of viruses is an essentially binary process. From these assumptions he created a formula in which the virus population is seen to grow exponentially. Using his estimation of virus growth, he then calculated the cost of the damage over a four-year period. If $25 must be spent per PC in addressing the virus problem then $1.25 billion will be spent over 4 - 5 years starting from last year if only 10% of the installation base of PCs are infected with only 10 viruses.

It is generally thought that the assumptions and the mathematics used are flawed and thereby the conclusions are incorrect. For instance, it is concluded that periodic scanning for viruses will increase the population of viruses instead of reducing it. Experience in Iceland, where the widespread use of Fridrik Skulason's antivirus led to a practical extinction of viruses for a while in that country, suggests the contrary (Skulason, 1990). There are also other indications that the mathematics may be oversimplified.

Kephart and White showed first that, given the assumptions made are correct, the conclusions are not correct (Kephart and White, 1991). They conclude that although the virus population will rise exponentially at first, it will reach saturation point or at least flatten as it becomes more difficult to find an uninfected PC. Scanning, or otherwise removing viruses, will result in the saturation level being lower and there is even a good chance of lowering the number of PCs infected. According to Kephart and White, Tippett's assumption that the "replication of viruses is an essentially binary process" is likewise incorrect. The statement implies there is homogeneous interconnectivity between computers. In fact, infections tend to be localised amongst a group of PCs. This slows the growth of infections even further.

One thing to note, however, is that even if the threat is not as bad as Tippett made it out to be, it is still to be taken seriously. There are at least 1400 viruses presently on the IBM-PC alone. Only perhaps 20% are definitely extinct or are research viruses, i.e. not in the wild. There are many very malicious viruses that will unrecoverably erase data and are hard to detect.

---

3 This was in response to a film about viruses we made with SWF television.

The effectiveness of scanners is becoming doubtful as the number of viruses grows daily and thereby the workload of the antivirus researchers. Today an antivirus can be seriously out of date within one week.

7.4 Why computer viruses are written

One of the most common questions asked by students in lectures is why computer viruses are written and by whom. Whereas the second question is simply answered, the former is by no means easy. From our experience at the Virus Test Center (VTC) and reports from Bulgaria (Bontchev, 1991), where virus programming seems to be a national pastime, virus programmers seem most commonly in their teens or early twenties, either still in school or college. Apart from that, there is little evidence that people in older age-groups are accountable for any known (i.e. distributed) virus. Exceptions to this are the cases of Joseph Popp[4], Mark Washburn[5] and the corporation Gliss & Herwig[6]. There are military projects worldwide dealing with viruses as a weapon and protection against viruses. There have been rumours about viruses being used in the recent Gulf War, but no evidence has reached us that this has happened[7]. There are no military viruses "in the wild" as far as we can tell. So, in some cases a motivation for programming a virus is known. But how about the rest?

One possible explanation is the search for fame and glory. If you cannot achieve fame, infamy will do. Programming a computer virus has too long been looked on as a major feat. A young programmer considers this as a proving ground to test his or her wings. If I can do this, I will be looked up to by my peers. If programmers are like artists in that they long for public recognition, virus programmers can be compared to graffiti artists. They wish their work to be widely seen. For this reason, subways are a popular canvas

---

[4] Joseph Popp of UK allegedly distributed a so called "Aids Information" disk worldwide. The program provided information on the (biological) HIV virus, but also encrypted the user's hard disk in the process. After being arrested in the USA and put on trial in the UK, he was recently set free by the Southwark Crown Court after a testimony by a London psychiatrist to the effect that Popp was psychologically unfit to plead (Wilding, 1992).

[5] Mark Washburn is the author of a whole series of viruses. The apparent reason for this activity is to create a virus that cannot be scanned for. These viruses are modifications of the Vienna virus so that they would be difficult, if not impossible, to search for by the normal string comparison method (scanning). He has apparently just finished his latest creation, V2P7 virus.

[6] This firm has an antivirus on the German market. They thought it would interest the public to have a "harmless" virus to experiment with so the virus was offered via advertisement in a German magazine. Due to strong protests from the rest of the antivirus community, the virus was removed from the "market".

[7] The recent report on "a computer virus being smuggled into Iraq on a printer chip which resulted in the screens of the air defence computers in Iraq to go blank" resulted from a journalist taking a InfoWorld April fool's joke seriously (*InfoWorld Magazine*, April 1st 1991).

for graffiti artists and similarly programming viruses is the method of choice for these programmers. Viruses, by definition, spread autonomously and widely. The action the virus carries is its "message", e.g. "look at this neat screen effect" or "I don't like you or I can take control over your PC". In some cases the interest in computer viruses is pure human curiosity. Although the virus property is not a useful programming technique per se, its resemblance to the biological virus fascinates many people. But, just as computers can hardly be compared with the complexity and adaptability of a human being, computer viruses cannot compare with the complexity of biological viruses or cells. Many serious researchers still see in the computer virus the path to "artificial life". For many people this is like "playing God in the computer" Many programmers attempt the task of programming a virus, just to see what it involves. As virus programming is not very difficult under MS-DOS, many succeed and for one reason or another let the virus escape.

7. 5 Legislation and computer viruses

7.5.1 Criminal law

Although most western countries have laws protecting property of various different kinds it seems to be difficult to apply these laws to computers. In some countries information is not considered property and is therefore not protected under law. In other cases the court views modification or destruction of the image on the magnetic media not to be punishable as the concept is too abstract. To extend the law to cover computer misuse, many countries have introduced specific laws dealing with computers.

In Germany, the "second law for fighting industrial crime" (§303a,b StBG, 2. Gesetz zur Bekämpfung der Wirtschaftskriminalität) was introduced. In section (a) of the law, the unauthorised modification of data, data media and data processing equipment is prohibited. There is much dispute about whether programs can be viewed as data. Moewes (Moewes, 1989) claims they can, but Gravenreuth (Gravenreuth, 1990) raises the concern that this would cause problems in applying the copyright laws to programs.

Section (b) of the law states that the rendering of an information system or its data useless is punishable. With respect to viruses, only viruses that either destroy data or overwrite the program it infects (rendering the program useless) comprise an illegal act. The intent must be clear for this law to be applicable. One problem remains in applying §303a,b to viruses. It is not clear whether the author can be held responsible for the actions of his virus when outside his or her direct control. There is no precedent case as of yet to resolve this issue.

Other laws can be applied to other virus problems. Product liability laws can be applied to cases where a product has been shipped infected with a virus. Copyright laws can used against the virus writer in some cases. In the UK the Computer Misuse Act was introduced in 1990 (HMSO, 1990). The act is divided into three sections, where the first and second apply mainly to hacking and fraud. Section 3, however, makes it an offence to modify computer material if unauthorised, where the intent and knowledge must be evident. The law applies also in an indirect manner, i.e. the author of the virus may be persecuted even if he has had no access to the computer in question. On the other hand, in the case of a benign virus the author may be able to dispute the intent to damage the computer. As of yet the law is untried, and a body of case law will be useful to see how exactly the laws may be applied (Ferbrache, 1992).

In the USA there has been much effort to make computer fraud and tampering a crime. Most states have either extended their laws or are considering doing so. The New York State Penal Code 156.20 and 156.25 (Computer tampering in the second and first degree) makes all unauthorised alteration or destruction of computer data or programs a crime. The wording is very general and could easily apply to a virus writer, as in the case of Robert T. Morris (the case is presently in appeal for his attack on Internet in 1988). Again, more precedent cases will be needed to define the scope of the law.

The California Penal Code 502 is, in contrast to the NYS-Pen-Code, very explicit. The Cal-Pen-Code defines various aspects of computers explicitly in detail, including "Computer Contaminant". Cal-Pen-Code 502 paragraph 8) subdivision c) states that it is a public offence to introduce a computer contaminant into any computer, computer system, or computer network. The problem with the Code is that the term "Computer Contaminant" is poorly defined and could apply to perfectly legitimate programs.

There was a proposal to introduce a federal "Computer Virus Eradication Act" which was eventually rejected. Rotenberg (Rotenberg, 1990) of Computer Professionals for Social Responsibility recognised that a virus may be a form of speech and therefore protected under the First Amendment. He criticised the various state laws for overreaching their goals or badly wording their codes. For instance, to penalise the "alteration of data" is ridiculous as any program will modify data in some way. Any program can "take control of the system resources" in some way or another. A bug in the program can cause very severe damage. There are great difficulties with coming to a satisfactory legal solution. Specific laws against computer viruses seems to be the wrong solution. Instead, the legislation should concentrate on unauthorised tampering, even without immediately apparent damage, to form a legal base against viruses.

Unfortunately, there will still remain the problem of finding and positively identifying the virus writer. In the few cases of known virus writers in Germany, the case had to be dropped for either lack of proof or lack of provable intent.

7.5.2 Example of the lack of legislation: Bulgaria

Bulgaria has the highest rate of producing viruses per capita than any other country in the world. How did this happen? The Communist Party in

Bulgaria decided to introduce computers to economic life in the early 1980s, with the intention of supplying computers to the USSR (now CIS). These were mainly clones of the Apple and the IBM-PC computers. The Bulgarian authorities did not introduce laws defining the ownership and protection of information and software. In fact, such a concept is foreign to Bulgaria and most of the former Eastern Bloc to this day. Would-be programmers could not sell their software as there were no laws preventing the copying of software to others free of charge. To make matters worse copying western software, modifying the copyright notice, removing the copy protection and reselling the pirated software to other former Eastern Bloc countries were all encouraged.

There were no economic reasons for introducing computers to a planned economy. If your goal is to fulfil the plan, why do it with less resources than necessary? What happened was that many PCs found their way into the hands of children and young adults who spent their time pirating software, playing the acquired games and exploring their "toy". When the idea of a computer virus was "imported" via hearsay and then actual working viruses, a new computer-based game was formed. This development was fed by the lack of identification of many of the programmers with their government and country. Frustration with their situation led many of them to program viruses in order to "get back" at their environment. The "Dark Avenger" is a prime example of this. His viruses are uncommonly destructive and infectious and he is notorious for distributing his creations worldwide via modems. It should be noted that this did not take much genius, but rather a malicious mind.

The public in Bulgaria often enough does not perceive viruses as anything more than a practical joke. There is little individual profit to be had with the data that is lost and the state seems not to care either (expressed in the lack of legislation), so why take the problem seriously? No action has ever been taken against a virus programmer. Bulgaria is an interesting study of a country where the lack of any feeling of citizenship has led to the irresponsible behaviour of the country's computer-literate population. It is to be hoped that the political reforms in Bulgaria also will result in social reforms.

7.5.3 The IFIP Resolution

On September 4th, 1989 at its international assembly, the International Federation for Information Processing (IFIP) issued the following recommendations with respect to computer viruses.

> *In view of the potentially serious and even fatal consequences of the introduction of 'virus' programs into computer systems, the Technical and General Assemblies of IFIP urge:*
>
> - *all computer professionals to recognise the disastrous potential of computer viruses;*

- *all computer educators to impress upon their students the dangers of virus programs;*
- *all publishers to refrain from publication of the details of actual virus programs;*
- *all computer professionals worldwide not to knowingly distribute virus code, except in controlled and laboratory environments, and all developers of virus detection and prevention systems to stop distribution of virus code for test purposes;*
- *governments, universities and computer system manufacturers to devote more resources to research into and the development of new technologies for the protection of computer systems, and government to take action to make distribution of viruses a criminal offence.* (IFIP, 1989)

Unfortunately, making the distribution of viruses a criminal offence is doomed to fail, at least with respect to virus writers, as few suspects will ever be found to be prosecuted. More progress is to be expected from preventing the open publication of virus code in any form (such as has been done by some leading antivirus "professionals"). This gives virus writing too much justification in the minds of young virus writers. If they see a virus published, it becomes acceptable to write one. As many published viruses are purposely simple, the virus writers will take it as a challenge to do better.

7.6 Ethics and computer viruses

We have seen in the previous discussion that legal efforts to curb the virus problem often fail or are ineffective. This is not all too surprising, as society has much catching up to do in order to grasp the effects of computer technology on people's lives. Moral standards and ethics have some advantages over legislation. Ethics can be set up by a group of professionals who are knowledgeable in their field. If they succeed in creating a widely accepted ethical standard this will give individual members of the community guidelines to act by. Hopefully this will improve the relationship of the profession to society. The lack of both ethical standards and legislation would leave us in the same position as Bulgaria is in now.

7.6.1 Professional ethics

Not all professional computer societies have a Code of Ethics. The German "Gesellschaft fur Informatik", for instance, does not have a Code, but is discussing it. IFIP has a special problem, as an international organisation it must consider the differences in cultures worldwide. For this reason IFIP is working on an ethical framework instead. Other Codes are weak with respect to malicious software, for example the British Computer Society's Code of Ethics. A good example of a Code of Ethics that addresses the problem of malicious software comes from the Association for Computing Machinery (ACM).

The "Code of Ethics and Professional Conduct" of the ACM is currently under revision (Anderson *et al.*, 1991). The present draft (No. 19) is a good example of an ethics standard that promotes good programming and design practices and the good relation of computer science to society. The draft contains four sections: (1) General Moral Imperatives, (2) Additional Professional Obligations, (3) Organisational Leadership Imperatives, and (4) Compliance with Code.

In section 1, general morals are discussed. In particular (1.2) (Avoid harm to others) is important with respect to malicious software. According to the guidelines accompanying the draft:

> *"Harm" means injury or any negative consequences, thus it prohibits actions within a computer system that result in unwanted harm to anyone: users, the general public, employees, employers. Such actions include destroying others files, crashing the system, and modifying programs that result in damage or serious loss of resources.*

Viruses have properties that violate this guideline. Viruses, by definition, modify programs without the user's consent. The resultant damage is apparent if you consider the number of files typically infected on a system. This means we have a serious loss of resources. Most often the virus will have side effects. These also can result in loss or damage of resources. Furthermore, a virus can have an intended function that is destructive. This is the most obvious violation. It has been argued that even normal programs can have side effects, and thereby violate the Code. However, it is standard practice to document known problems if these are not easily resolved. The user of the software may then decide whether or not to run the risk. The user, however, has no influence over whether or not a virus installs itself on his/her system.

The guidelines further state:

> *Unintended action, for instance, negligent computing, may also lead to harm. It is our opinion that in such an event that the person or responsible party is obligated to undo or mitigate the negative consequences caused unintendedly or unknowingly. Only few virus writers are actually known, whereas the author of a legitimate program always is. Virus writers dodge their responsibility by hiding behind a cloud of anonymity.*

7.6.2 Hacker ethics

There is a myth amongst the older hackers[8] that the entire hacker community abides by a set of eternal ethical rules as set out by Levy (Levy, 1984) in 1983. These "rules" set forth a rather playful attitude toward computers, but also an anti-authoritarian philosophy. Under such a code of ethics, the writing of viruses and passing them around is not only allowed, but even encouraged. In

[8] In this context the term "hackers" can apply to both those who are dedicated to computers and to those who break into computers.

this, and other things, the hackers afford themselves a lack of compassion for normal computer users who are not as fortunate in understanding the technology as well as they do, and are often the sufferers.

Interestingly enough, when the "Chaos Computer Club" of Germany translated Levy's hacker ethics, they added one rule, non-existent in the original (Chaos Computer Club and Wieckmann, 1988). This states that the hackers were not to trash people's data. This stands in contradiction with writing and distributing viruses, as only a few are completely benign. Unfortunately this rule never seemed to impress any hacker. The Chaos Computer Club published one of the first viruses and to this day will send you a copy of the virus for the asking. To their defence, they also tried to help users in need, when hit with a virus.

7.7 Conclusion

Computer viruses are a serious threat not only to PCs but also to larger systems. Security mechanisms and organisational means can help to detect and prevent viruses, but generally cannot guarantee security from the virus threat. The impact of viruses, which are growing exponentially in number, could cause enormous damage. Criminal laws to fight the writing or publication of virus code, necessary to increase the awareness of the virus threat, have been shown to be insufficient.

We need ethical standards and educational means to teach potential virus programmers and institutions how to use information technology responsibly. Unfortunately, not all national or international computer societies have published ethical codes that can be applied to forbid the programming and publication of malicious computer software. Especially young computer users in schools and in universities should be taught about computer ethics, the impact of system vulnerabilities and how to use computers responsibly. Furthermore, institutions must learn what kind of security mechanisms and organisational means should be taken to most effectively prevent threats such as malicious software.

References

Anderson, R. E., Denning, P., Engel, G., *et al.* (1991) ACM code of ethics and professional conduct, revision draft No. 19 (9/19/91). *ACM SIG Computers & Security*, **21**(2-4), October 1991.

Bell, D. E. & LaPadula, L. J. (1973) *Secure Computer Systems: A Mathematical Model.* Mitre Corporation, Bedford, Mass.

Biba, K. J. (1977) *Integrity Considerations for Secure Computer Systems.* USAF Electronic Systems Division, Bedford, Mass., April 1977.

Bontchev, V. (1991) The Bulgarian and Soviet virus factories. *Proceedings of the First International Virus Bulletin Conference*, Jersey, UK, August 1991.

Brunnstein, K. & Fischer-Hübner, S. (1990) Risk analysis of 'trusted' computer systems. In: *Proceedings of the 6th International IFIP TC 11 Security Conference on Information Security (Sec'90)* Helsinki, May 1990.

Brunnstein, K., Fischer-Hübner, S. & Swimmer, M. (1991). Concepts of an expert system for computer virus detection. In *Proceedings of the 7th International IFIP TC 11 Security Conference on Information Security (Sec'91),* Brighton, May 1991.

Chaos Computer Club & Wieckmann, J. (eds) (1988) *Das Chaos Computer Buch.* Rowohlt Verlag GmbH (Wunderlich).

Clark, D. D. & Wilson, D. R. (1987) A comparison of commercial and military computer security policies. In: *Proceedings of the IEEE Symposium on Security and Privacy.*

Cohen, F. (1986) *Computer Viruses.* PhD thesis, University of Southern California.

Ferbrache, D. (1992) *A Pathology of Computer Viruses.* Springer Verlag, New York.

Gasser, M. (1988) *Building a Secure Computer System.* van Nostrand Reinhold Company, New York.

Gravenreuth, G. (1990) Computer Viren und Ähnliche Softwareanomlitäten. In Seminar & Workshop, *Computer Viren.* Viren-Service Hamburg, perComp-Verlag GmbH, December 1990.

HMSO (1990) *Computer Misuse Act 1990.* HMSO Publications Centre.

IFIP (1989). *Worldwide warning on computer viruses.* Press statement, San Fransisco, September 1989.

ITSEC (1991) *Information technology security evaluation criteria (ITSEC),* provisional harmonised criteria.

Kephart, J. O. & White, S. R. (1991). Commentary on Tippett's "The kinetics of computer virus replication". *Proceedings of the Fourth Annual Computer Virus & Security Conference,* March 1991.

Levy, S. (1984). *Hackers.* Bantam Doubleday Dell Publishing Group, Inc.

Moewes, K-H. (1989). Computer-Viren und verwandte Anomalien - betrachtungen eines kriminalpolizeilichen Sachbearbeiters. In: M. Paul (ed.) *GI- Jahrestagung I,* Munchen, October 1989.

Rotenberg, M. (1990). Prepared testemony and statement for the record on computer virus legislation. *Computers & Society,* **20**, 1, pp.12-25, March 1990.

Skulason, F. (1990). Speech at the first and founding meeting of EICAR, December 1990.

Tippett, P. S. (1991). The kinetics of computer virus replication. *Proceedings of the FourthAnnual Computer Virus & Security Conference,* March 1991.

U.S. Dept of Defense (1985) *DoD trusted computer systems evaluation criteria,* DoD 5200.28-STD. Washington D.C.

Wichers, D. R., Cook, D., Olsson, *et al.* (1990). PACL's: An access control list approach to anti viral security. In *Proceedings of the 13th National Computer Security Conference,* Washington D.C., October 1990.

Wilding, E. (1992). Popp goes the weasel. *Virus Bulletin,* January 1992, pp. 2-3.

8

Jacques Berleur

What is happening now with technology assessment?

The *concept* of technology assessment (TA) seems to have appeared in 1962, in a NASA study for the American Academy of Arts and Science. It was elaborated to evaluate the potential fallouts or repercussions of the conquest of space in the domain of peaceful and scientific uses. Ten years later, the OECD stressed, in its 1971 report *Science Growth and Society*, the increasing gap between the rhythm of technological innovations and the capacity of society for a development in harmony with its social goals and objectives. In appearance, the concept would seem to have changed, but in reality it fits very well with what it has become today.

We would like, in this paper, to examine the concept of TA and its history, in order to show that most probably the history of the concept is at the same time the history of its institutionalisation. We will then evoke the different functions and methods of TA, as they appear now and question the links between these different methods and functions before concluding on the main issues which have been achieved 30 years after the concept first appeared.

8.1 Some definitions

A rather old definition given by the United States Office of Technology Assessment stated that "Technology Assessment is a kind of research which gives to those who are responsible for policies a set of coherent information. In other words, it is a system which allows us to raise questions and to obtain correct answers in due time. Technology assessment distinguishes and defines the most important problems, evaluates the different possible modes of action and presents conclusions. It is a method of analysis which systematises the nature, importance, impacts and advantages which are related to some technological progress."[1]

---

1 US Congress, House Committee on Science and Astronautics, *Technical Information for Congress,* Report to the Subcommittee on Science, Research and Development, Legislative Reference Service, Library of Congress, 90th congress,

Twenty years later, The Netherlands Organization of Technology Assessment (NOTA) wrote: "The definition of Technology Assessment to which NOTA subscribes is the entirety of activities and methods used therein for the earliest possible study of the various aspects and consequences of a technical or scientific development for (different groups of) the population, preferably in their mutual connection, for the sake of finding the suitable role in society for the technology or scientific disciplines concerned."[2]

Recently, Petrella, Head of the FAST Programme[3], expressed his view according to his experience of more than 12 years in the field: "By Technology Assessment, I mean the set of procedures and specific means that a society gives to itself in order to understand the issues at stake and the very nature of the development and of the present and potential use of a given technology and in order to assess its economic, social and political consequences in the short and long term."[4]

More and more, TA tries to shed light on the fact that there is no innovation without consideration of, at least, a three-dimensional perspective: scientific and technological, economic and organisational, social and societal. We have called it, according to the FAST culture, the "Technology Assessment Triangle" or, better the "TA Pyramid" since these three dimensions are oriented towards a vertex, which indicates the decision-making and taking policy process: see **figure 1** below.

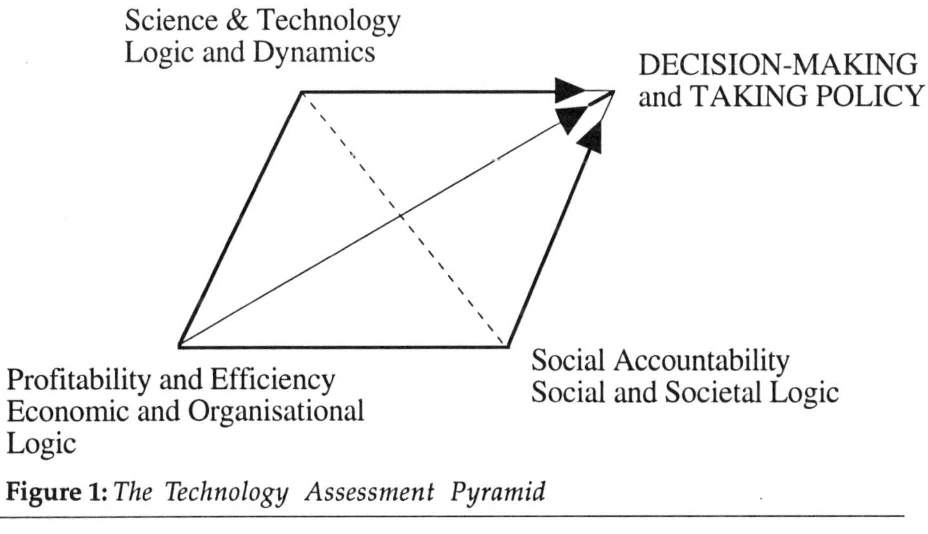

Figure 1: *The Technology Assessment Pyramid*

1st session, US. Government Publishing Office, August 1968.

[2] *EURETA Newsletter*, European Regional Technology Assessment, CEC, Brussels, 1, January 1988, p. 7.

[3] FAST, Forecasting and Assessment in Science and Technology, is a Programme which started in 1979 in the DG XII of the Commission of the European Communities.

[4] R. Petrella, Les enjeux du Technology Assessment. *Journal de Réflexion sur l'Informatique*, Namur, n°18, December 1990.

8.2 Technology assessment as an institution

Before the institutionalisation of TA in different countries in specific offices associated with legislative or executive bodies, several workshops, symposia or conferences took place where the need was felt to go further in setting up those institutions. Table 1 mentions the most important ones.

Workshops, Symposia and Conferences	
1972	The Hague, First Congress of the International Association for Technology Assessment (ISTA)
1976	Second Congress of ISTA in Ann Arbor
1982	Congress of Bonn, at the initiative of West Germany Ministers of Interior and of Research & Industry
1987	First CEC Congress on Technology Assessment, Amsterdam, (ECTA-1)[5]
1990	International Federation for Information Processing (IFIP-TC9), 4th International Conference on Human Choice and Computers, Dublin: *Information Technology Assessment* [6]
1990	Second CEC Congress of Technology Assessment, Milano, (ECTA-2)[7]
1992	Third CEC Congress of Technology Assessment, Copenhagen (ECTA-3)

Table 1: *Workshops, Symposia and Conferences*

At the European level, we must add the exciting activity of the FAST Programme (Forecasting and Assessment in Science and Technology). Since 1979[8], this Programme, conducted inside of DGXII of the Commission of the European Communities, produced a particularly large list of publications but, moreover, really created a network of researchers throughout all the Member

---

5 *Technology Assessment. An Opportunity for Europe,* S.C. de Hoo, R.E.H.M. Smits & R. Petrella (eds), Publication of the Dutch Ministry of Education in co-operation with the Netherlands Organization for Technology Assessment (NOTA) and the Commission of the European Communities, The Hague, September 1987. Volume 1: *Proceedings,* 305 pp.; volume 2: *Full Papers,* 328 pp.

6 *Information Technology Assessment,* J. Berleur & J. Drumm, editors, Proceedings of the 4th IFIP-TC9 International Conference on "Human Choice and Computers", jointly with the CEC-FAST Programme, Elsevier Science Publishers B.V., North-Holland, 1991.

7 *People and Technology. Ways and Practices of Technology Management,* Milano, Italy, 14-16 November 1990. The Commission of the European Communities in Co-operation with the Italian Ministry of University and Scientific and Technical Research.

8 Decision of the Council of Ministers of July 25th, 1978. See Journal Officiel des Communautés Européennes, n° L225/40 (August 16, 1978).

States with a real "TA spirit"[9] . This Programme is still active inside the so-called MONITOR Programme.

8.3 The institutionalisation of TA

The example of the US Office of Technology Assessment is certainly at the origin of the proliferation of similar institutions in Europe, but with more than ten years delay. The discussions in the different countries are remarkably concentrated between 1983 and 1989, as is shown by the dates of the creation of the different national institutions: see Table 2 below.

1972	USA, Law creating the "Office of Technology Assessment" (**OTA**) close to the American Congress[10]
1983	France, Creation of the "Office parlementaire d'évaluation des choix scientifiques et technologiques" (**OPECST**)[11]
1984	The Belgian Flemish Regional Council creates the "Stichting Technologie Vlaanderen" (**STV**), which in 1986 was attached to the Flemish Economic and Social Council
1986	The creation of two offices: one in Holland, the "Nederlandes Organisatie voor Technologische Aspectenonderzoek" (**NOTA**), the other in Denmark, **TeknologiNævnet,** the "Danish Board of Technology"
1987	The European Parliament establishes the "Scientific and Technological Options Assessment" (**STOA**), and the same year, the United Kingdom its Parliamentary Office of Science and Technology (**POST**)
1988	The FAST Programme reinforces its network by setting up the "European Network of Technology Assessment at Regional Level" (**EURETA**)
1989	Germany, after extensive discussion establishes the "Büro für Technikfolgen-Abschätzung des Deutschen Bundestages" (**TAB**), depending upon the "Ausschuß für Forschung, Technologie und Technikfolgen-Abschätzung des Deutschen Bundestages" (Bundestag Committee for Research, Technology and Technology Assessment).
1992	Will this be the date of the birth of Belgian Walloon "Office of Coordination of Technology Assessment" (**OCTA**)? History will tell us, but the process is well on the way.

Table 2: *Timetable of the Institutionalisation of TA*

[9] The list of Publication of FAST-1 (1978-1983) may be found in: *Eurofutures - The Challenges of Innovation*, Butterworth & Co., London, 1984. A summary of research projects of FAST-2 (1984-1987) may be found in the 2 volumes published by the Commission, DG XII/H/2, *European Futures, Prospects and Issues in Science and Technology*. A first list of FAST-3 is available at the Commission since December 1st, 1991.

[10] Technology Assessment Act, Public Law 92-484, 92nd Congress, Oct. 13, 1972.

[11] Loi n°83-609 du 8 juillet 1983, led to the creation of a delegation named 'Office parlementaire d'évaluation des choix scientifiques et technologiques' (OPECST).

This intensive feeling for the necessity of institutionalising TA in the form of support from parliamentary or executive authorities is also reflected in less ambitious projects. The Commission of Science and Technology of the Council of Europe, with the aim of helping the political decision makers, has for instance organised parliamentary and scientific trips and conferences (for example, Helsinki in 1980 and Tsukuba in 1985) which may be considered as a unique approach for reflecting on the improvement of parliamentary decision processes about scientific and technological questions and, in particular, about the optimal use of information technologies vis-à-vis the democratic process.

8.4 Functions of TA

In the practice of TA, and in the arguments favouring it as well as in the literature, some *eight functions* have been distinguished by Leyten and. Smits, which do not exclude each other and which often overlap[12] .

1. *Reinforcing the position in the decision process*: this alludes particularly to the TA initiatives of parliaments, but also to other political and policy-oriented actors who, by reinforcing their information-base on scientific and technological developments, try to gain a greater influence in the decision-making process.
2. *Supporting the short and medium-term policy of the government* (executive and legislative branch) through which thought can be given within the framework of the existing policy to the investigation of alternatives, evaluation and, not infrequently, legitimisation.
3. *Contribution to the development of long-term and future governmental policy* by supplying information about possible developments and alternatives.
4. *Early warning*, oriented towards supplying information about the potentially problematic and undesirable consequences of technological developments at the earliest possible stage.
5. *Broadening knowledge and decision-making* by supporting social groupings in the formulation of their own strategy in respect of technological developments.
6. *Tracing, formulating and developing socially desirable and useful technological applications (constructive TA).*
7. *Promoting the acceptance* of technology by the general public.

---

12 John Leyten and Ruud Smits, A Revival of Technology Assessment: The Development of TA in Five European Countries and the U.S. In: S.C. de Hoo, R.E.H.M. Smits & R. Petrella (eds), Technology Assessment, An Opportunity for Europe, Publication of the Dutch Ministry of Education and Science in co-operation with the Netherlands Organisation for Technology Assessment (NOTA) and the Commission of the European Communities (DGXII)/FAST, The Hague, Government Printing Office, September 1987.

8. *Advancing scientists' awareness of their responsibility to society.* These eight functions identified by Leyten and Smits would seem to give a reasonably complete picture. In addition to these only the following relatively new functions were mentioned at the 1987 Amsterdam ECTA-2 Congress: "assisting in the priority of national and international research programmes and monitoring relevant developments in other countries, implying a potential contribution towards stimulating the international learning process."[13]

8.5 TA methods

To assume the mentioned functions, some twelve methods for undertaking TA may be found in the literature or in the practices of TA Offices[14] .

1. *The available literature analysis* which is not very original and may be considered as the starting point of any research project. But, what is searched is the accumulation of partial results and an international comparison. This allows the creation of significant statistical series or the increase of hypotheses to be tested.
2. *The comparative study of statistics series* may be used to make "retrospective" analysis of the determining factors in a well specified innovation process, for instance. It also allows "prospective" and forecasting analyses, but the limits of such prediction are well known. We can mention: the availability of data on long periods; the co-variance between two series is not necessarily a relevant explanation; the "explanations" are most often controversial (see for instance the series on "employment and new technologies", etc).
3. *Studies by questionnaires or interviews of people affected by the new technologies. Research by survey.* We can mention the analysis of diffusion of innovation in Italian industry (1980-1985) conducted by the CNR in which 35,000 firms were involved. This study has been updated in 1990. The *Eurobarometer* survey conducted at the European level lists the ranking of European interests, the sensitivity of the public to science and technology in general, a global measure of knowledge, the confidence in science and technology, etc.[15]
4. *Case studies* are also used in TA methods. The difference with survey methods is that case studies provide us with detailed and in-depth studies. Let us mention the "Brighton Study" on the adoption of the new

---

13 Ruud Smits, *State of the Art of Technology Assessment in Europe,* A report to the 2nd European Congress on Technology Assessment, Milano, 14-16 November, 1990.

14 First Biennial Report to the European Parliament, on the Social and Economic Implications of New Technologies (ASSESS Group, FAST-CEC DGXII, November 1990).

15 ibid. Annex II.

technologies by the private sector managers: 150 companies have been contacted.

5. *Experts' advice on the new technologies* is a well known method among the "prospectivists". The real problem is their "usual" disagreements! But, even if there is a consensus, how is it reached? Are there not dominant people? The most well-known method is the DELPHI method - where the experts give separate advice without being together and reacting in a second round to a summary of their answers in the first one. The Nominal group method differs from DELPHI in the fact the experts are together at the same place.
6. *The method of scenarios* is surely one of the methods which fits very well with the functions of TA as they were enumerated. It consists in forecasting and predicting the possible futures and in determining relevant factors and their relations to existing data analysis. Let us mention the study of the NEDO (National Economic Development Office) on the potentialities of information technologies for the UK (1987).
7. Robert Junk & Neubert Müllert have suggested and experienced the *"Future Shops"* method, where there is no reference to specific expertise, but where the emphasis is put on sharing of experiences, visions, plans by groups of around twenty citizens. The reference is to shared values. Phases of such Future Shops are: preparation, experience sharing, development of vision of the future, feasibility evaluation and action.
8. *Consensus Conferences* are amongst the oldest specific methods of TA. They are already mentioned in experiences reported by the USA OTA, but a kind of renewal may be found in the Danish experience. The audience is around 100-200 participants along with 10-12 experts and 10-15 "lay people". The latter are selected after advertisement in newspapers and prepare themselves during two weekends. The consensus report is written during the three-day Consensus Conference. After a short presentation by the experts' group, an analysis of the proposals is made by the "lay people" who write the consensus report. This may be corrected by the experts (but only any major scientific errors) and is then presented to the media. Consensus Conferences in Denmark are held in the surroundings of the Parliament so that politicians may get "some flavour" of what is discussed and happening! Let us give some examples of themes which have been tackled: Biotechnologies and Agroindustry, Food Irradiation, Genetic Engineering, Air Pollution, etc. The idea of a Consensus Conference is not to reach a full agreement about a specific issue, but "to make clear on which points agreement can be reached and on which there are conflicts"[16].

---

[16] TeknologiNævnet, Consensus Conference on Food Irradiation, Final Document, 22-24 May, 1989. Some of the mentioned characteristics of the Danish experience emerge from personal discussion with Jørn Ravn, General Secretary of

9. *Social Experiment in real situations.* Everyone is probably familiar with the French experiment on MINITEL, but other experiments are today being undertaken. Let us mention the Danish "Community Experiments with Information Technology" where 16 projects where launched in 1985-86, controlled by the local population and where around 50,000 participants were involved. The total budget was DKr 30 million (i.e. approx 4 million Ecus)[17]. There are surely limits to such experimentation *in situ*: the assessment criteria are difficult to clarify and quantify, as recognised by many researchers[18]. But the advantages are predominant: we are facing *proactive* TA and the intertwining of social organisation and technological development may be really clarified.
10. *Scientometric Methods*, like *Leximappe* where databases of technical and scientific papers are analysed, allow the discovery of associated words (co-occurence) and thematic networks of researchers. The content of research, its structure, and its evolution, the emergence of new problematics, of possible restructuring are enlightened so that "proactive" TA is made possible. It may also be considered as a tool of analysis and follow-up of scientific production.
11. *Systems and socio-technical networks analyses* are also considered as TA specific methods. They include: the *socio-technical systems analysis* (e.g. the analysis of delays in the innovation development which authorises a *reverse salient*); the *socio-constructive analysis* (the technical objects get their significance only in their relationship to informed social groups); the *socio-technical networks analysis* (the technical objects are always defined and re-defined in their translation and innovation networks).
12. We must also mention the *Schema of C. Limoges* which mixes constructive analysis (genesis, development, structure of the technology), implementation analysis (precise study of the interactions technology/society), prospective analysis of impacts which serves as decision support to social and political conditions of the implication of new social actors[19] .

Speaking of methods, we must mention more classical methods like *Cost-benefit, Cost-advantage Analyses* including risk assessment analyses, multi-

---

TeknologiNævnet. See also, Torben Agersnap, Gurli Jakobsen & Jeanne Kempinski, *Vurdering af en konsensus-konference*, TeknologiNævnet, 1989.

17 See Tarja Cronberg, *Experiments into the Future. A Summary of Results from Danish Experiments with Information Technology*, Copenhagen, Finansministeriet, 1990, 30 pp.

18 See Lars Qvortrup, *Social Experiments with Information Technology and the Challenges of Innovation*, Dordrecht: Reidel, 1987.

19 C. Limoges, De la technologie comme objet problématique à l'évaluation sociale des technologies, in: *Diffusion des nouvelles technologies: Stratégies d'entreprises et évaluation sociale*, Montréal, Ed. Saint-Martin, 1987.

criteria methods, etc. In practice, some TA institutions make use of external research centres, but there is always a "Position Paper" of the Board (for example the US OTA allocates one fifth of its budget to external research). Some are also very sensitive to the implication of involving different groups, as the social partners, and favour "Popular edition" for public debates. TeknologiNævnet supports local debates with material (publications and films), names of resource-people, finances (Dkr 3000/as incentive), etc.

8.6 Link between function and methods

In Table 3 we summarise the relationship between the functions of TA and the most appropriate methods which could be linked with them. This is only an attempt that does not pretend to be exhaustive and does not correspond explicitly to the mode of operation in the different TA Offices. It is more a theoretical suggestion to be explored further.

From experience and case studies

Let us now mention some of the case studies in which we are involved and briefly evoke some of the problems which are raised or some remarks emerging from our experience in the field.

ISDN

ISDN is most probably a commercial reality facing competitive private networks (e.g. SWIFT) and in search of users. TA studies must follow the historical description of its development, the general technological context, the precise "map of actors", their profiles, their bargaining power, etc. In this case, we meet problems of "social experiment", but with an *ex post* analysis which will enable an *ex ante* prospective view of a continuous evaluation process.

Patient or Medicard

The Patient Card or Medicard is a good example of *ex ante* TA : there are only, at present, social experiments *in situ*. What will those "cards" be? Medical files? Patient files? Identification cards? Successes or failures of experiments will determine their content.

If they were really in the hand of the patients, they could help them to be more aware of their own health situation through the access to "medical platforms" where they could question specific, well designed, databases. What appears now to be clear is the necessity for transparency of potential uses, for the definition of the objectives and goals, and an equal effect on the market between supply and demand. One of the major difficulties is the capacity of the actors to anticipate the problems which will be raised by such innovation.

Videotex

Most of the TA studies on Videotex have raised questions such as : Who has been promoting the idea? Who is doing the TA research and financing it?

TA studies face the dilemma of two logics: technical on the one hand, and socio-organisational and socio-political on the other. Most of the time, TA studies support one of these and emphasise dimensions such as productivity, efficiency or rate of use. But there are very few qualitative data about: "Who is the real user?", his/her behaviour, his/her satisfaction, etc. Here again, there is no transparency either on the goals or on the results.

F4.		*Early warning*
	M1.	Available literature analysis
	M2.	Comparative study of statistics series
	M5.	Experts advice on the new technologies
	M10.	Scientometric Methods
	M11.	Systems and socio-technical networks analysis
F1.		*Reinforcing the position in the decision process*
F5.		*Broadening knowledge and decision-making*
F6.		*Tracing, formulating and developing socially desirable and useful technological applications (constructive TA)*
F7.		*Promoting the acceptance of technology by the general public*
	M7.	"Future Shops"
	M8.	Consensus conferences
	M9.	Social experimentation in real situation
F2.		*Supporting the short- and medium-term policy of the government (executive and legislative branch)*
F3.		*Contribution to the development of long-term and future governmental policy*
	M2.	Comparative study of statistics series
	M3.	Studies by questionnaires or interviews of people affected by the new technologies. Research by survey
	M4.	Case studies
	M6.	Method of scenarios
	M8.	Consensus Conferences
F7.		*Promoting the acceptance of technology by the general public*
	M2.	Collect of information and of knowledge
	M3.	Implication of the different groups, of the social partners.
	"Popular edition" for public debates	
	M4.	Support of local debates
F8.		*Advancing scientists' awareness of their responsibility to society*
Better if associated with :		
	M3.	Studies by questionnaires or interviews of people affected by the new technologies. Research by survey
	M4.	Case studies
	M9.	Social experimentation in real situation
F9.		*Assisting in the priority of national and international research programmes and monitoring relevant developments*

	in other countries, implying a potential contribution towards stimulating the international learning process
M1.	Available literature analysis
M2.	Comparative study of statistics series
M3.	Studies by questionnaires or interviews of people affected by the new technologies. Research by survey
M6.	Method of scenarios
M9.	Social experimentation in real situation
M10.	Scientometric methods
M11.	Systems and socio-technical networks analysis

Table 3: *Summary of Functions of TA and Methods linked with them*

Companies

Most often, companies are absent from the TA field. If there is any TA, it is rather informal, through some strategies of social re-appropriation of occurred changes and by deviation of uses. Or, it is a marginal negotiation of already defined projects, an "adaptation" more than an evaluation.

But, companies are today facing the uncertain relevance of some computerisation projects with organisational, economic and social issues; they need tools and methods to manage this uncertainty, in terms of defining projects (upstream from the "life cycle" of the project or during its implementation [social experiment, etc.]). This means that clear and democratic rules have to be defined, socially legitimised and accepted.

The feeling of a greater awareness of the necessity to anticipate (due to complexity and context of uncertainty) is increasing. And that is a challenge for TA: what can it propose in opposition to economic, technical and organisational efficiency? what could be a "social efficiency"?

The specificity of TA, in the reported cases, may be stressed in terms of democratic rules (well informed actors ... or users), supporting institutions, methods, etc.

8.7 The balance after 20 years of TA

Let us conclude by mentioning some of the highlights of TA today: a researchers' community exists with conferences, workshops, and published debates; a set of specific institutions, attached to legislative or executive authorities, are more and more related in networks; awareness among the public is growing on some more sensitive questions. One may understand that there is a shift which is taking place from "Computers and Society" to "Society and Computers". But, many questions remain: Will companies be interested in it? Is TA a "tool for users"? Will we be able to face the increasing process of globalisation?, and so on.

The *basic issue* at stake is the *socialisation of TA* which means that the functions and practices of TA have to be integrated into the decision process and in the choices about any technology development. There are also five more *specific issues* at stake[20].

(1) TA has to be recognised, in terms of the acknowledgement of its institutions; there is still defiance and mistrust of it from the industrial and financial world, scepticism from political authorities and a rather weak awareness among the general public.

(2) TA has to succeed in the process of institutionalisation, i.e. to gain or win political credibility (to involve industry is one of the major difficulties for this credibility).

(3) TA must avoid any instrumentalisation, i.e. any appropriation by the experts, or the Minister, or any other. Constructive TA may help. In its Dutch meaning, it is a continuous process of TA, but in a broader sense, in the EEC meaning, it would have to start from problems and not from technology, raising questions like: "For such a problem that we have to solve, which are the technologies available by means of which we shall have the best solution?"

(4) We have to develop TA networks but mainly in the sense of "multiple approach", "multiple sectors", and "multiple places".

(5) Finally, we must reinforce the globalisation awareness. TA must be culturally inscribed in the context of the globalisation of the economy and in the context of the unity of mankind. Let us call it the "Butterfly effect". When a butterfly is browsing in Brazil, it affects the taxi-driver in Stockholm!

[20] R. Petrella, Les enjeux du Technology Assessment, op. cit.

9

Chrisanthi Avgerou & Shirin Madon

Development, self-determination and information

9.1 Introduction

In recent years, much has been written and said about information and information technology being vital resources in promoting socio-economic development for third world countries (UN, 1986; Munasinghe, 1989). It is often pointed out that lack of data and limitations of the capacity to apply advanced scientific models hinder development planning efforts, inefficiencies of information processing in government and industries prohibit economic growth, inadequate capacity to participate in world-wide communication systems implies isolation and backwardness. Consequently, increasingly more attention is given to information and "knowledge"-intensive techniques for alleviating social problems and raising the economic value of production processes. Declining capital cost and rapid improvements in hardware and software technology make possible the diffusion of information technology in even the poorest countries (Kluzer, 1990).

However, there is also considerable scepticism regarding the efforts of developing countries to adopt information-intensive procedures and to exploit the developmental potential of information technology. Indicatively, Lind (1986) questions whether the promise of benefits from information technology is nothing but a myth and argues that unrealistic expectations have led to the failure of information technology applications. Hill (1988) makes the point that the introduction of new information technologies drawn from modern industrialised society implies cultural values that are fundamentally at variance with those of traditional societies.

In this chapter we examine how the current emphasis on information activities affects the self-determination of developing countries and their people. First, we review the general theoretical arguments regarding information-handling activities and development, which drive the dominant trends towards information-intensive societies, the "informational mode of development" (Castells, 1989). Then we outline the conceptions of development which are relevant to the poor countries of the world. We identify self-determination as a fundamental aspect of development and suggest two relevant levels for consideration: the level of nation states, and the level of individual citizens and their immediate communities, such as the village. We discuss how the informational mode of development affects the self-determination of developing nations and social groups within them, and what governments and organisations could do to avoid risks and to achieve potential benefits.

9.2 Theoretical perspectives on the significance of information and IT for development

The terms "information age" and "information economy" have been coined to convey the prevailing perception that nations tend to devote increasing proportions of their effort to information handling. Specifically, the term information age is used to express the contention that in business, policy making and public life in general, information has now acquired a role more prominent than ever before. There are efforts to measure the information intensity of a society by measuring the amount of information it circulates and processes (Hamelink, 1984). Better known are the efforts to measure the information economy in terms of the proportion of occupations concerned with the creation and handling of information (Muchlup, 1962; OECD, 1986), or in terms of the contribution of the production of information goods and services to the national accounts of a country (Porat, 1977; OECD, 1986; Karunaratne, 1984; Engelbrecht, 1986; Katz, 1986).

The continuing growth of the measures of these indicators is hardly disputed. What is much more controversial is the explanation of these trends and their relation to development. The most influential view is that the trend of growing information activities observed in the industrialised economies in the post-war period signifies the arrival of the post-industrial economic stage. The notion of transformation of the economy from an industrial to a service-based post-industrial economy has been described by Bell (1973) and other writers but rests upon a much older model of linear economic change known as the Fisher/Klark thesis. This thesis views economic growth as a succession of growth and decline of the three economic sectors: primary, consisting of agriculture, forestry, and fishing; secondary, consisting of manufacturing, construction and utilities; and tertiary, which consists of services. The argument is that, as economies grow, rising productivity levels, made possible by technological advances, allow workers to pass to the next sector and, as national incomes rise, the increase in demand generated is channelled first into the secondary sector and then into the tertiary sector.

Bell's model expresses a similar linear succession by referring to pre-industrial, industrial and post-industrial phases. In the post-industrial economies, human and information services, such as health, education, recreation, research and development, hold a prevailing position. Bell considers theoretical knowledge to drive innovation and change and to give rise to new social relationships and new structures. He calls theoretical knowledge the "axial structure" of post-industrial societies. Knowledge and information are strategic resources for the transformation of the economy and professional and technical groups are considered to be catalysts of change. The post-industrial economy, it is argued, is a new kind of economic system which does not preserve the economic structures of the industrial economies. The driving forces cease to be ideological; they are knowledge and logical reasoning.

Many writers in the 1970s and the 1980s have disputed the logic of the post-industrial economy thesis. For example, the argument about the growing demand for services has been challenged by Gershuny and Miles (1983), who put forward the view that the trend is towards a "self-servicing" economy which substitutes goods for services. People tend to use new products to service themselves, as for example, the use of television programmes or videos to deliver material for higher education, instead of the labour-intensive conventional teaching methods. Gershuny explains the increase in service occupations in terms of changes in the technological and organisational structure of production within manufacturing industries. Thus, the increase in service occupations such as managers and technicians became necessary in order to increase the efficiency of the production of goods. The growth of service industries is explained as an organisational phenomenon, with manufacturing industries subcontracting services to specialised service companies.

Central in this thesis is the role of technological and organisational change (Gershuny and Miles, 1983). The connection between technical innovation, economic development and social and institutional change has been studied extensively (Schumpeter, 1939; Freeman *et al.*, 1982; Hall and Preston, 1988) establishing relations between the pervasiveness of certain types of technologies with periods of radical change in the structure of the economy. Technologies are characterised as "pervasive" if their applications affect almost all sectors of the economy. More specifically, a technology has pervasive economic effects and employment implications if it generates a wide range of new products and services, reduces the costs and improves the performance of the processes, services and products of many sectors of the economy, it gains widespread social acceptance (although new regulatory frameworks are needed), and generates strong industrial interest as means for profitability and competitive advantage (OECD, 1988). Indeed, information technology is singled out as being at the centre of the present wave of technological change in most industrialised countries. The interconnected innovations in integrated circuits, computer hardware, software and telecommunications affect dramatically the cost of storing, processing, communicating and disseminating information. Also, they lead to new industries producing a great range of new products and services.

Another line of critique of the post-industrial notion challenges the view of the emergence of a new economic system. According to Mandel (1975), the growth of the service industries is driven by the search for profits. Shifts in employment follow shifts in investment in the service sector; the post-industrial era is viewed as the continuation of the capitalist system by further extending the technical division of labour. Morris-Suzuki (1988) argues against both the theses of Bell and Mandel. She views the changes occurring in Japan, one of the most industrialised countries, as the transformation to a new form of capitalism, which she calls "information capitalism".

Theoretical arguments such as the above do not highlight only the differences of perception of the writers; by focusing on different aspects of the nature of the occurring socio-economic changes they contribute to the formulation of more elaborate theories. One recent attempt to understand the geography of socio-economic change draws from a great number of concepts and theoretical constructs from different writers (although without discussing their theoretical origins and bypassing relevant critical or controversial issues) to formulate an interesting set of hypotheses (Castells, 1989). First, advances in information technology and the emergence of information processing as the fundamental activity conditioning the effectiveness and productivity of the processes of production, distribution, consumption and management have led to a new mode of development, called "informational mode" or "informationalism". Second, the emergence of the informational mode has coincided with fundamental changes of the capitalist system in its efforts to overcome its structural crisis. Third, informationalism and capitalism have converged in a process of techno-economic restructuring of the society. On the basis of this set of hypotheses Castells examines a variety of themes, such as the locational pattern of information technology and information-technology user industries, the significance of the military use of information technology, and the impact of information technology on employment, capital-labour relations, the social and spatial restructuring of cities and regions, and the internationalisation of the economy.

9.3 Development and the notion of self-determination

While the debate on the nature of changes that characterise economic growth and social reforms in industrialised societies continues, efforts for the development of the poor countries of the world focus on different sets of issues. In the economic literature of the early post-Second World War period, the process of development was conceived of primarily in terms of the structure and growth of the national economy and the degree of development was most often measured in terms of national income (Easterlin, 1968). It was assumed that less developed countries should aspire to achieve the type of society which existed in the developed world. In order to do this, it was believed that they would have to pass through a number of stages of economic growth similar to those which the countries of western Europe has experienced (Rostow, 1960). Emphasis was placed on stimulating the "take off" which would be needed to launch developing countries into this process of economic growth and much emphasis was placed on industrialisation and urbanisation in developing countries.

In the 1960s, however, this dominant view of development as economic growth came to be challenged and different approaches to the process of development emerged. There was a redefinition of the goals of development with much greater emphasis on non-economic aspects. There was increasing evidence to suggest that while a few developing countries managed to increase their growth rates and restructure their economies, the majority were not able to achieve such results. Moreover, the economic growth that did occur was accompanied by a variety of social and political problems (Conyers and Hills, 1984). Hence, development came to be conceived of and measured not only in economic terms, but also in terms of social well-being and political structures as well as in terms of the quality of the physical environment (UNDP, 1991). This led to the emergence during the 1970s of the "basic needs" approach to development which was reflected in the development policies of a number of third world nations. In India, for example, considerable importance and priority was attached to the Minimum Needs Programme in the 1970s which included the provision of elementary education, health, water supply, roads, electrification, housing and nutrition (Bhattacharya, 1982).

There has been a major re-evaluation of the obstacles to development and the causes of underdevelopment. Experiences in many parts of the developing world during the 1960s and 1970s led to the realisation that underdevelopment was not caused merely by lack of resources, capital or skills, but also by the nature of relationships between groups of population in a country or between nations. Within developing countries, it was noticed that the adoption of development policies which favoured the poorer groups of the population was often hampered because the power to make and implement such policies rested with an affluent minority. This line of thought has been influenced by dependency theories (Amin, 1974; Amin, 1976; Rodney, 1972) which raised the issue of self-determination of developing nations from two points of view. First, in terms of empowering the poor within a country with basic rights to human development. Second, in terms of the ability of independent nation states to make decisions within the prevailing international power structure.

In many developing countries, the attainment of political independence had created the illusion of having a greater measure of self-determination over their own destiny. However, while colonialism was perhaps an extreme form of dependence, barriers to self-determination took more subtle forms based on the international division of labour (Roxborough, 1979). Self-determination was only realisable insofar as these countries had a strong voice in decision-making processes governing the volume and direction of economic activity within their territory. This was a great challenge because of the unequal exchange relations between rich and poor countries with the latter dependent on the former for capital and technical progress to equip their industrial sectors (Cardoso and Faletto, 1979; Mabogunje, 1989).

A major contributing factor to dependency was seen to be the overwhelming role of the powerful multinational corporations. The multinationals increased their grip on the raw material and labour power of developing countries which resulted in increasing concentration of capital and the integration of production on a world-wide basis. Nevertheless, most developing countries envisaged that multinationals would be instrumental in introducing technology adapted for domestic use, creating employment, as well as providing know-how (Dosa, 1985). This expectation did not materialise except in a few cases. The multinationals, by giving emphasis to highly sophisticated and capital intensive production methods, neither provided new skills, nor the opportunity to adjust technology to local needs. Without the development of local capabilities, no long-range benefits could be acquired and it became difficult for developing countries to bridge the wide technological gap between their nations and the developed world thereby underscoring the reality of economic dependence (Mabogunje, 1989).

In summary, the main perception of development as economic growth has been challenged by alternative approaches which, in addition to economic growth, have given much emphasis to social and human aspects of development. Attention has been focused on the notion of dependency between citizen's groups and between nations as a fundamental aspect of underdevelopment. As governments and private companies of advanced industrial countries are able to extend more effectively and articulate their activities on a global scale, there is the growing prospect of many developing countries becoming more dependent on foreign economic and political interests. New information and communication technologies emerge as a major force presenting new opportunities but also bringing to the surface the critical issue of the self-determination of developing countries, both in terms of the ability of independent nation states to make decisions within the prevailing international power structure, and in terms of preserving the basic rights to human development of individuals within those countries.

9.4 Information related trends and the self-determination of developing countries

Concerns about the risk of losing national sovereignty as a result of lagging behind other countries in effectively utilising information and the emerging powerful information and communication technologies have been repeatedly expressed, even in industrialised countries (Nora and Minc, 1980; Murphy, 1986). Military strength, political independence, cultural identity, as well as economic competitiveness, depend on a country's capacity to generate, acquire, handle and disseminate information. Not surprisingly, the emerging powerful information and communication technologies, which are instrumental in such activities, have become a significant aspect of government policy (English and Watson Brown, 1984; Trade and Industry Committee, 1988).

While industrialised countries are making great efforts for the development and production of such technologies, for the establishment of rich information infrastructures, and for the promotion of information intensive activities, developing countries are faced with unprecedented opportunities, but also new threats. The impressive economic success of newly industrialised countries such as Singapore, Korea, Hong-Kong and Taiwan, are often quoted to indicate the developmental opportunities of information intensive industries. Since the 1970s large developing countries such as India and Brazil have worked out policies to safeguard and promote indigenous information technology industries, to develop their own information resources and to encourage the utilisation of information in order to serve national development goals (Zimmermann, 1990). Several studies indicate that information technology is increasingly widely diffused in almost all regions of the world (Kluzer, 1990; Kaul *et al.*, 1989), promising solutions to chronic pressing problems (such as bureaucratic inefficiency), providing the means to participate in industries with universal standards (such as airlines or banking), or even providing new opportunities (such as monitoring geological and climatic changes by remote sensing technologies). The scope of this section is to examine some of the major issues related with the intensification of information-related activities and the self-determination of developing countries.

Media communication

Mass media and telecommunications have undoubtedly great developmental potential. Many countries have used mass media for emancipatory, educational and nation building purposes. A well known example is the project SITE, which used satellites to reach and educate remote communities in India (Morison, 1987). Indonesia has also used satellite communications, since the early 1980s, to reach its many islands and to create a common national identity (Kayatme, 1983).

However, the international scene is characterised by severe disparities in information and information technology. This problem started being discussed in the mid-1970s. The debates on a "New International Information Order" culminated in the MacBride Commission report (1980). The report heavily criticised the contemporary network of global telematics that reinforces dependency relationships (Jayaweera, 1990). A call was made for a democratic restructuring of global information opportunities. It was suggested that industrialised countries and transnational companies should help in the creation of self-determined communication institutions in developing countries, by exercising restraint in exploiting the virtual one-way flow of information, advertising, political propaganda, and mass media content. Perhaps the most important outcome of the New International Information

Order was the increased recognition that a crucial dimension in international relations is the degree of influence on decision-making and consequent participation in information exchange.

However, after publication of the MacBride Commission report, little actually changed in the 1980s. International information services and communications beyond the control of developing countries perpetuated cultural hegemony because the values of the industrialised countries had greater opportunity for transmission. The inability of poor societies to produce quality programmes for filling up enormous airtime meant that national networks have no option but to buy cheap productions from salesmen.

Brazil is widely cited for the great progress it has made in developing a telecommunications structure that has been helpful in maintaining its national and cultural integrity (Fadul and Straubhaar, 1991). The evolution of cultural industries in Brazil, at least in the area of television, has been an important factor in limiting the influence of the multinationals. More recently, there have been pressures to decentralise and regionalise the media, especially television. It is hoped that with the strengthening of regional or local media, there will be an expansion of communications access to those sectors of the population that are still not reached by television. This decentralisation therefore is expected to have important cultural implications because it would enable the various regional identities to come to the surface and play a stronger role in the development of national culture. Despite these positive trends, however, Fadul and Straubhaar argue that the Brazilian culture still continues to be threatened by pressure from industrialised countries, especially the USA.

The commodification of information

One of the most significant changes that has occurred in recent decades is the emergence of a market for information services. The new industry of information services involves a chain of activities: the production and collection of "raw data", the storing and organisation of data in databases, the processing of available data to meet particular informational needs of clients, and the provision of telecommunication network facilities to access required data. This chain of activities is usually composed by several actors: the "raw data" provider, the database host, the information processing service provider, and the telecommunication network operator. The most widely traded information is financial data, scientific abstracts, and bibliographic data (Hamelink, 1984; O'Brien & Channing, 1986).

The availability of such information services provides an easy - albeit expensive - solution to the severe lack of information and information processing capacity that many developing countries face. Access to scientific databases, such as those on agriculture, can provide information which is lacking from the libraries of national universities, research institutes, and ministries undertaking development programmes. Although most poor countries lack the capacity to process data as required by development projects, they may have their data processed in international information services centres. Moreover, many developing countries can enter this new market as data providers. Data about their products, their resources, their culture have value as a tradable commodity.

However, each of these opportunities bears significant risks of dependency and unequal exchange. Access to scientific data centres of industrialised countries may provide a temporary solution for particular development programmes, but cannot be a substitute to an indigenous infrastructure for generating and utilising such data by local experts. Despite efforts by international agencies, such as the UNESCO programmes UNISIST or PGI, the development of such an infrastructure has so far proved particularly problematic (Avgerou, 1992).

Also, even if a country has raw data to sell, the value-added chain of the information industry is unfavourable to the data providers. The most profitable part of the chain is the storing and processing of data (Hamelink, 1984). Yet, at present, the vast majority of countries are raw data suppliers, with the USA, and to a lesser extent Europe and Japan exclusive exporters of processed data (Sauvant, 1986). As it is becoming cheaper in many cases for enterprises in developing countries to send their design problems, calculations, research and routine data abroad rather than to form local teams, developing countries risk the transfer of key decision-making processes (Bessant, 1990) outside their own decision-making centres. The commodification of information appears to reinforce the unequal exchange that development theorists have long ago observed as a major problem hindering development.

Overall, lacking adequate resources to fund the development of an indigenous information sector or to purchase information goods and services in the international market-place increases the vulnerability of developing countries regarding the management and control of their own resources. A developing country may have to face the prospect of buying information on the state of its own natural resources from a multinational company.

The diffusion of information technology

Developing countries come to rely increasingly on technologies which are produced almost exclusively in industrialised countries. As Rada (1980) wrote, electronics is becoming the heavy industry of the future and will be an essential sector in the development of "knowledge-intensive" economies. However, most developing countries have no capacity to produce information technology and very limited ability to maintain and upgrade locally the imported technology. For many years, international aid agencies have been the main providers of information technology for projects in developing countries. However, support from international agencies has tended to be sporadic and uncoordinated and has often created great problems in terms of compatibility and parts (Schware and Choudhury, 1988). Few international aid agencies have policies concerning the use of information technology in developing countries (Dow, 1986). Donor agencies treat computers and information technology as tools that support projects in other traditional aid-receiving sectors such as agriculture, energy, health and transport. They do not consider information technology as a new and important sector in itself requiring integrated rather than *ad hoc* support (Munasinghe, 1989).

There is increasing concern that the role of international aid agencies as carriers of information and information-handling resources for development will cause more dependency between developing and developed countries. Odedra (1990) notes that in the case of many African countries, equipment is brought into countries through aid agencies without the necessary imparting of knowledge of how to use, operate or maintain it. Hence, very little information technology transfer has actually taken place to date between the developed world and the African developing countries.

Information systems for development planning

There have been many efforts by governments of developing countries and international agencies to address the building of information resources such as document referencing systems, management information systems and statistical information services (Heitzman, 1990; Avgerou, 1992). Technical information emerged as a prime requirement for strengthening a developing country's economic and industrial base and science and technological document centres cropped up under international, especially UNESCO, sponsorship (Dosa, 1985). Also, in recent years, a number of developing countries have attempted to create computer-based information systems similar to those in operation in the institutions of industrialised countries to support the planning and implementation of development programmes. For example, in India, district planning is being introduced in the states with the National Informatics Centre placing microcomputers in each of the 439 districts (Sanwal, 1987). In Kenya, the Resource Management for Rural Development Project is currently engaged in the introduction of microcomputers in the districts (MPND, 1987). In South-east Asia, Malaysia is extending its Integrated Development Project Information System (SETIA) to the districts (Han and Render, 1989).

With all these initiatives, however, the main objective of improving the planning and monitoring systems of rural development remains unfulfilled (Sanwal, 1990). Avgerou (1992) notes that current efforts to create information systems infrastructure for development planning assume a particular rationality of the decision-making process using numerical analysis and quantitative data which is at odds with the dynamics of organisations in developing countries. They ignore the significance of political influences which stem from their social and cultural environment. However, the extent to which development planning relies on political and informal channels of information and decision-making practices has implications for the kind of information and information processing required for development planning. In Madon's (1992) research on the impact of the Computerised Rural Information Systems Project (CRISP) in India, the findings revealed that the CRISP system design has been based on a rational model of planning perceived by the central government which was at variance with the reality of informal decision-making that prevailed at the district level. The system was designed and developed with inadequate understanding of the functioning, dynamics and causes of inefficiencies in the bureaucracy. As a result, in many occasions the system reinforced, rather than alleviated, bureaucratic inefficiencies.

Waema and Walsham (1990) also make the point that such applications predispose those who use them to the acceptance of values, attitudes and norms of the society in which they originate. For example, the principles observed in the rational model of planning are based on reasoned decision-making and logic. In other cultures, the basis of decision-making is more judgmental, based on intuition (Felts, 1987).

More recently, there has been growing recognition amongst planners that while information and communication is a factor in development, the causes of underdevelopment are mostly structural. Madon's (1992) findings reveal that information technology may be a vehicle for promoting structural change within the administration. National and state governments began to encourage greater local communication and information-sharing as part of a larger policy of investment in rural areas and local autonomy in contrast to earlier models of control from the centre and fascination with high-tech tools.

9.5 Information developments and the self-determination of the poor

In addition to deepening dependency linkages between countries, recent trends of information development also affect the self-determination capacity of the unprivileged poor communities within developing countries. While a great deal has been written about using the potential of information technology for spreading the benefits of socio-economic development to weaker sections of the population in developing countries (WHO, 1987), in practice such applications are rare. On the contrary, a standard feature of societies in developing countries has been an elitisation of information with a concentration of schools, libraries and technology in relatively few and mostly urban centres. In this section we examine briefly how the current information developments affect the human development in poor countries.

Most information systems applications for development leave the masses of individuals in rural areas uninvolved in the process of socio-economic development. The case of the CRISP project in India, mentioned above, demonstrates how the formal information system which is intended to serve the needs of the poor results in cutting off the beneficiaries, and their immediate village communities from the decision-making process of the development programme. CRISP was based on a model of a desirable - to the originators of the scheme - democratic decision-making, whereby a village community decides by democratic procedures which of its members are in most need to receive credit assistance from the rural development programme. This idea, however, ignored some deeply rooted traditions such as decision-making by authority rather than through participation of all. It also ignored differences of perception and priorities of "needs". The attempt to impose a "fair" and effective decision-making process resulted in the complete alienation of the beneficiaries from the information system. Contrary to the assumed logic of the designed information system, decisions at this local level follow the traditional values of the community, and information supplied to the district administration as input to CRISP is largely unreliable. As a result, the task that the system was built to perform, namely the monitoring of the development of the poorest within the rural communities, is based on arbitrary information.

The effort to develop an overall national capacity for effective information handling tends to have a discriminatory effect, favouring the most prosperous population of urban areas and those with a western type educational background, against the poor and the traditional communities (Aksoy and Goddard, 1990). Scarce financial and technical resources lead to a concentration of training efforts in urban centres, creating a further distinction between an elite capable of making a living in an information intensive society and "backward communities" which are increasingly marginalised from the centres of power.

Discrimination between communities in the same country is not a new phenomenon. Previous industrialisation efforts have had similar effects and led to the movement of "appropriate technology". The current efforts to build the skills and the infrastructure of a "post-industrial society", do not raise the same degree of opposition because they do not have the immediately obvious effects devastating to the fabric of the community, such as mass exodus from rural communities to the cities or environmental destruction. They have, nevertheless, subtle but far-reaching effects on the rationality and cultural values (Mowshowitz, 1980) of traditional communities and can aggravate the conflict between "modern" and "traditional" which is already discernible among the communities of many developing countries.

Some attempts have been made by governments in developing countries to popularise informatics culture into the lifestyles of the common public. For example, the project GISTNIC (General Information Service Terminal) in India was introduced in 1991 by the National Informatics Centre to provide online information to the public. GISTNIC is currently available throughout the country in booths located at public places both in urban and rural areas (NIC, 1991).

There are few endeavours to promote local projects aiming at overcoming cultural biases inherent in imported technology and to develop information resources that meet the needs of users. Notable examples are the adaptation of portable microcomputers to villages where it reaches relatively small audiences (Dosa, 1985) and Forster's (1990) primary health sector data collection and expert system for community health workers.

9.6 Conclusions

This chapter has explored some of the issues facing developing countries which are brought about by the increasing significance attributed to information. The concurrence of threats and opportunities represents a policy dilemma which developing countries have to face in preserving their right to self-determination. The fundamental difficulty for developing countries is that they try to participate in the international system, which tends to impose imperatives on information handling models for decision-making, while preserving their rights and capacity for their self-determination. In addition, large numbers of individuals and communities within these countries tend to be further marginalised as their traditional life pattern is considered inadequate for coping with the demands of the emerging information intensive and technologically demanding post-industrial society, and they have little means to develop the new skills required.

So far little effort has been made to study what information processes are required and are feasible of being developed in developing countries. Our current knowledge and dominant practices regarding the handling of information is the result of research mainly in North America, North Europe, Japan, and Australia. Although there is little evidence that this knowledge is applicable to the conditions of the rest of the world, particularly those of Eastern European countries, South European countries and third world countries, it is applied unquestionably as a recipe for economic success. This situation puts further obstacles to development, hinders the exploitation of the developmental potential of information technologies and promotes dependence rather than inter-dependence among nations. Characteristically, in the literature on information systems the term "globalisation" has acquired the meaning of networking the globe to serve the interests of multinational corporations. Even if one has faith in the benevolent nature of such economic institutions and the trickle-down effect their success may have for the poor nations within which they do business, a vital aspect of development, that of self-determination is neglected. At present, internationalisation trends enabled by new information technologies are based on the domination of a single culture, a single system for valuing information, and a single rationality for decision-making.

In order to preserve their right and capacity for self-determination, developing countries have to address themselves to their own informational needs and to develop their own information order. There have been several initiatives to break the western monopoly of the knowledge industry by encouraging regional projects involving developing countries with much in common. For example, in terms of database access, Saracenic *et al.* (1985)

reported that a large percentage of scientific research relevant to developing countries comes from other developing countries, although such data formed a small part of sources in western-produced databases. In this connection, the advent of the South Asian Association for Regional Cooperation (SAARC) and other regional policy bodies may form the backbone for future developing countries' initiatives in information technology. Many of the African countries have also recently been participating in regional cooperation ventures for the development of broadcasting and communications infrastructure (Mabogunje, 1989). In order to strengthen attempts to apply information technology to the problems and situations in developing countries, Aksoy and Goddard (1990) have called for developing countries to broaden the scope of their information policy framework to incorporate not only issues concerning the technology itself, but also issues concerning uses of the information and alternative ways of delivering information services.

Finally, international agencies should reconsider their policy of unquestioned promotion of information processing according to models applied in industrialised countries. Informational development is of crucial significance in the era of "information economies" and they should begin to support research and development projects intended to understand and support the information needs in developing countries.

References

Aksoy, A. & Goddard, J. B. (1990) Mobilising information resources for economic development. A report for the World Bank. University of Newcastle-upon-Tyne. Centre for Urban and Regional Development Studies.

Amin, S. (1974) *Accumulation on a World Scale: A Critique of the Theory of Underdevelopment.* New York: Monthly Review Press.

Amin, S. (1976) *Unequal Development: An Essay on Social Formations of Peripheral Capitalism.* New York: Monthly Review Press.

Avgerou, C. (1992) Information systems for development planning. *International Journal of Information Management.* forthcoming.

Bell, D. (1973) *The Coming of the Post-industrial Society.* Heinemann, London.

Bessant, J. (1990) Information technology and the North-South divide in information technology. In: R. Finnegan *et al.*, (eds) *Information technology: Social issues.* Open University, Milton Keynes.

Bhattacharya, V. R. (1982) *New Face of Rural India.* Metropolitan Book Company, New Delhi, India.

Cardoso, F. H. & Faletto, E. (1979) *Dependency and Development.* (Translated by Marjory Mattingly Urquidi) University of California Press.

Castells, M. (1989) *The Informational City, Information Technology, Economic Restructuring and the Urban-Regional Process.* Blackwell, Oxford.

Conyers, D. & Hills, P. (1984) *An introduction to development planning in the third world.* John Wiley and Sons, Hants.

Dosa, M. (1985) Information transfer as technical assistance for development. *Journal of the American Society for Information Science*, **36**, pp. 146-152.

Dow, M. (1986) *Review of selected donor agency policies on computers and informatics in Third World countries.* Third World Academy of Science, Study Group on Computers and Informatics for Development, Trieste, Italy, January 8-10.

Easterlin, R. A. (1968) Overview on economic growth. In: D.L. Sills (ed.) *International Encyclopaedia of the Social Sciences* , **4**, New York.

Engelbrecht, H. (1986) The Japanese Information Economy: Its Quantification and analysis in a Macroeconomic Framework (with Comparisons to the U.S.). *Information Economics and Policy,* **2**, pp. 277-306.

English M. & Watson Brown, A. (1984) National Policies in Information Technology: challenge and responses. *Oxford Surveys in Information Technology*, **1**, pp. 55-128.

Fadul, A. & Straubhaar, J. (1991) Communications, culture and informatics in Brazil: The current challenges. In: G. Sussman and J. Lent (eds) *Transnational communications - Wiring the third world.* pp. 1-27, Sage, London.

Felts, T. (1987) The development of information systems in the third world. MSc. Dissertation, London School of Economics.

Forster, D. (1990) Health Informatics in Developing Countries: An analysis and two case studies. PhD Thesis, London School of Economics.

Freeman C., Clar, J., & Soete, L. (1982) *Unemployment and Technical Innovation: A study of Long Waves and Economic Development*, Frances Pinter, London.

Gershuny, J. I. & Miles I. D. (1983) *The New Service Economy: the Transformation of Employment in Industrial Societies.* Frances Pinter, London.

Hall P. & Preston P. (1988) *The Carrier Wave - New Information Technology and the Geography of Innovation 1846-2003*, Unwin Hyman.

Hamelink, C. J. (1984) *Transnational data Flows in the Information Age.* Chartwell-Bratt, Sweden.

Han, C. K. & Render, B. (1989) Information systems for development management in developing countries. *Information and Management,* **17,** pp. 95-103.

Heitzman, J. (1990) Information systems and development in the third world. *Information Processing and Management,* **26,** pp. 489-502.

Hill, S. (1988) *The tragedy of technology.* Pluto Press, London.

Jayaweera, N.D. (1990) Communication satellites: a third world perspective. In: R. Finnegan *et al.* (eds) *Information technology: Social issues.* Open University, Milton Keynes.

Karunaratne, N.D. (1984) Planning for the Australian Information Economy. *Information Economics and Policy,* **1,** pp. 345-367.

Katz, R.L. (1986) Explaining Information Sector Growth in Developing Countries. *Telecommunications Policy,* Sept, pp. 209-228.

Kaul, M., Patel, N. & Shams, K. (1989) New Information Technology Applications for local development in Asian and Pacific Countries. *Information Technology for Development,* **4,** 1, pp. 1-10.

Kayatme, S. (1983) The prospects of Electronics and Telecommunications in Indonesia. Presented at the Indonesia - US seminar on Science and Technology, Washington D.C. 3 - 5 October 1983.

Kluzer S. (1990) Computer Diffusion in Black Africa: A Preliminary Assessment. In: S. Bhatnagar and N. Bjorn Anderson (eds) *Information systems for development.* North-Holland, Amsterdam.

Lind, P. (1986) Computers, myths and development. *Information Technology for Development,* **1,** pp. 99-117.

Mabogunje, A.L. (1989) *The development process - A spatial perspective.* Unwin Hyman, London.

MacBride, S. (1980) *Many voices, one world : Communications and society, today and tomorrow.* Unipub, New York.

Madon, S. (1992) The impact of computer-based information systems on rural development : A case study in India. PhD. Thesis, Imperial College of Science, Technology & Medicine, London.

Mandel, E. (1975) *Late Capitalism.* New Left Books, London.

Morison, P. (1987) Information Technology in the Third World and Patterns of Development. MSc dissertation, London School of Economics.

Morris-Suzuki, T. (1988) *Beyond Computopia - Information, Automation and Democracy in Japan.* Kegan Paul International, London.

Mowshowitz, A. (1980) Ethics and Cultural Integration in a Computerized World. In: A. Mowshowitz (ed) *Human Choice and Computers,* 2. North-Holland, Amsterdam.

MPND (1987) Semi-annual report no. 3 : Resource management for rural development project. Ministry of Planning and National Development, Nairobi, Kenya.

Muchlup, F. (1962) *The production and distribution of knowledge in the United States.* Princeton University Press.

Munasinghe, M. (1989) *Computers and informatics in developing countries.* Butterworths.

Murphy, B. (1986) *The International Politics of new Information Technology.* Croom Helm, London.

NIC (1991) *GISTNIC - General Information Service Terminal National Informatics Centre,* Planning Commission, New Delhi, India.

Nora, S. & Minc, A. (1980) *The computerisation of society : A report to the President of France.* The MIT Press, Cambridge, Mass.

O'Brien R. C. & Channing, M. (1986) The global structure of the electronic information services industry. *Oxford Surveys in Information Technology,* **3**, pp. 175-210.

Odedra, M. (1990) *The transfer of information technology to developing countries.* PhD thesis, London School of Economics

OECD (1986) *Trends in the Information Economy.* Information Computer Communication Policy, **11**.

OECD (1988) *New Technologies in the 1990s. A socio-economic Strategy.* Paris.

Porat, M. U. (1977) *The Information Economy: Definition and Measurement.* Washington DC, US Department of Commerce/Office of Telecommunications.

Rada, J. F. (1980) *The Impact of Microelectronics,* International Labour Organisation, Geneva.

Rodney, W. (1972) *How Europe underdeveloped Africa,* Bogle-L'Ouverture Publications, London.

Rostow, W.W. (1960) *The stages of economic growth, A non-communist manifesto,* Cambridge University Press.

Roxborough, I. (1979) *Theories of underdevelopment.* Macmillan Educational Ltd, London.

Sanwal, M. (1987) *Microcomputers in development administration.* Tata McGraw-Hill Publishing Company Limited, New Delhi, India.

Sanwal, M. (1990) End user computing in development administration : The vital role of administrators. *Public Administration and Development,* **10** , 221-232.

Saracevic, T., Braga, G. M. & Afolayan, M. A. (1985) Issues in information science education in developing countries. *Journal of the American Society for Information Science,* **36**, 3, pp. 192-199.

Sauvant, K. P. (1986) *International Transactions in Services: The Politics of Transborder Data Flows,* Westview Press, Colorado.

Schumpeter, J. (1939) *Business Cycles.* McGraw-Hill, New York.

Schware, R. & Choudhury, Z. (1988) Aid agencies and information technology development. *Information Technology for Development,* **3**, 2.

Trade and Industry Committee (1988) *First Report on Information Technology,* HMSO, London.

UN (1986) New Information Technologies and Development. *Atas Bulletin,* **3**.

UNDP (1991) *Human Development Report.* UNDP, Oxford University Press.

Waema, T. M. & Walsham, G. (1990) Information systems strategy formation in a developing country bank. *Technological Forecasting and Social Change,* **38**, pp. 393-407.

WHO (1987) *Enhancement of transfer of technology to developing countries with special reference to health.* Advisory committee on health research. World Health Organisation, Geneva.

Zimmermann, J-B. (1990) Information Technology Policies for Developing Countries facing a World-Wide Information Technology Industry. In: S. Bhatnagar and N. Bjorn Anderson (Eds.) *Information systems for development.* North-Holland, Amsterdam.

10

Mayuri Odedra

Enforcement of foreign technology on Africa: its effect on society, culture, and utilisation of information technology

10.1 Introduction

In the past few years, the importance of information technology, especially computers, has been greatly emphasised in Africa and other developing countries (Rada, 1985; Bennet and Kalman, 1981; Tottle and Down, 1983). The acquisition of computers, both in the public and private sectors, has increased tremendously, despite the scarce foreign exchange to buy the equipment and the high import duties imposed on data-processing equipment. The types of machines used and their applications vary in sophistication from country to country, but a major growth, in both acquisition and utilisation of computer equipment, has taken place in the last decade (Odedra, 1990).

Yet, despite the rapid growth, the amount of technology which is effectively being transferred to the indigenous people of these countries is small and the under-utilisation of equipment has increased. Often, under-utilisation is blamed on lack of skilled computer personnel or foreign exchange to buy spare parts. Research done by the author, however, shows that there are other more important reasons, including the roles of management, international organisations, suppliers, and education and training facilities that influence under-utilisation (Odedra, 1990).

Computerisation in Africa started in the late 1950s and early 1960s during the colonial period. The first computers were installed in the government, mainly to assist in preparing financial records, tabulation, computing statistics, and processing government accounts, payroll and pensions (see various country profiles in *Information Technology for Development: an International Journal*, Oxford University Press). As the administrative jobs were becoming more labour intensive, automation had to be introduced. The larger multinational corporations started introducing computers soon after that, followed by private financial organisations. The growth in the number of computers installed was steady but slow until the late 1970s. From early 1980s onwards, the number of computers installed increased substantially for a number of reasons.

Firstly, the major reduction in hardware and software prices and the availability of sophisticated micro- and personal-computers with large processing and memory capability made access to such technology possible for many more users who could not afford the equipment earlier. Secondly, the international aid organisations started donating computers to these countries and expatriate consultants began using computers in their projects themselves; these computers were usually left behind when the project was finished. Thirdly, bilateral aid organisations and other funding bodies, such as World Bank and International Monetary Fund (IMF), insisted that the recipient countries start making use of the technology in order to organise and manage their data and information better. Lastly, the suppliers saw a small but potential market in Africa and started setting up shop. They saw the beginning of a computerisation trend and started taking advantage of the little computer literacy and awareness that exists amongst management in Africa.

Most of the reasons outlined above for the rapid growth in the number of computers are either directly or indirectly influenced by the so-called "foreign forces". This term is used here to refer to all foreign organisations, personnel, technology, and knowhow. The organisations include international organisations such as the United Nations (UN) organisations, World Bank and IMF, multinational corporations and suppliers. The personnel referred to are largely expatriate consultants. The technology includes both hardware and software researched, developed and produced abroad. Below, the role played by these forces is examined further in detail and its impact on the African continent, and the society at large, analysed.

10.2 The role of foreign forces on Africa

The various foreign forces have played a major role in introducing information technology to Africa. Over the years, they have kept the African nations "up-to-date" with new developments. Initially, the colonials introduced computers in the public sector to help them with their data processing. Then came the large multinational corporations (MNCs) which made use of the technology in compliance with their headquarters. The local companies, having similar business operations and interests as the MNCs, were therefore forced to introduce automation in order to keep up with the competition. Later came the international organisations who either donated equipment and provided technical assistance or, for various reasons, forced the organisations to introduce automation.

So far, from the various forces outlined above, international organisations such as USAID, CIDA, SIDA, UNESCO, UNIDO and UNDP have been the most important agents for introducing this technology to Africa. For example, by the mid-1980s, half of Africa's computer installations consisted of aid donated equipment. In 1989, over 80 per cent of the computers in the Zimbabwean government were donated (Odedra, 1990). This shows the importance of such organisations in influencing the African information technology (IT) market.

Ensuring successful transfer of technology, however, has received little or no attention within these agencies and there are indications in some instances that this transfer process is already faltering, preventing or complicating the effective use of the technology (Schware and Trembour, 1985). Computer equipment is frequently given to an organisation with no training or provision for extra recurrent costs. Many of the organisations cannot afford such costs and therefore simply store the equipment. Moreover, a majority of foreign aid is tied to the donor country's products and consultants. Organisations have to accept what they are given. This leads to a choice of developed countries' capital intensive technologies, even in cases where more appropriate technologies are available. Overall, the international organisations have increased the dependency of the African countries on the more advanced countries by donating unfamiliar equipment which requires not only spares from abroad but also foreign consultants (Odedra, 1993).

The three other groups of organisations which have played a significant role in introducing and enforcing IT to Africa are the suppliers of the technology, the MNCs as users of the technology, and other international technical and development assistance organisations. As mentioned earlier, the suppliers have seen a potential market and have come with their wares to take advantage of the situation. Many of the internationally well known manufacturers and suppliers that have set up shop in Africa are notorious for manipulating management and decision-makers into buying their equipment, providing very poor after-sales service, especially maintenance and training, and often providing obsolete technology. Their main concern is in selling "boxes" at inflated prices and not in transferring technology.

Most MNCs operating in Africa are users of the technology and this has often forced their local counterparts to acquire the technology, either because of reasons of competition or as a status symbol. Usually the local organisations rush into buying the technology without giving much thought to their needs and capabilities to sustain the technology. The results are often disastrous.

A third group of organisations has also contributed to the current situation in Africa. In the early 1980s, bilateral aid and donor organisations, mainly the IMF and World Bank, complained of the poor information systems the Africans held, especially those to do with expenditure monitoring (Brodman, 1986). These organisations therefore forced African governments to introduce automation in order to have an effective way of monitoring their finances. The outcome of such initiations has not always been that anticipated. Systems have often been introduced without identifying the real needs or organising the skills or data to be processed.

Foreign personnel have also played a very important role in influencing the IT industry in Africa. In most donor-assisted projects, technical assistants, mainly expatriate consultants, are provided with the donated equipment. Although most African countries suffer from lack of computer-skilled people who would be able to manage projects, especially at senior level, expatriates are employed even in cases where such skills were locally available. Overall, because of the "foreignness" of the technology, the scarcity of education and training facilities in the country (Botelho, 1992), the slow growth in utilisation, and the little importance given to the technology (and consequently on human resource development) at the national level so far, the African countries suffer from lack of computer-skilled personnel.

This has meant that foreign personnel have to be brought in to do the work. The problem with such consultants and foreign staff is that they take little interest in learning about the organisation in which they are placed to introduce computers. They either do not have the time or are not willing to learn about the social and cultural issues of a country, apart from when it comes to sight-seeing. They show little interest in passing on the knowhow and skills to the potential users. As many consultants are not familiar with the local requirements and conditions in these countries, they usually end up designing poor systems which are under-utilised.

Overall, the "force" playing the key role in all this is the technology itself. Most the technology used in Africa originates from the advanced countries. As the technology is developed for the Western market, it is not always suitable for the different culture (the way of life of a particular society or group of people, including patterns of thought, beliefs, behaviour, customs, traditions, rituals, dress and language) and infrastructure in Africa. Often, inappropriate technologies that tend to be capital-intensive and make limited use of existing capabilities and resources in Africa are transferred. In a few countries where locally developed or assembled machines and locally produced software packages exist, little use is made of these technologies, even when these technologies are much cheaper to buy than those imported. The reasons again are largely inflicted by the foreign forces. Organisations would rather use foreign technology for status reasons. Moreover, the foreign forces have brainwashed the local users about the poor quality of such products, and foreign technology therefore dominates Africa in such a way.

Together with the physical equipment brought in from abroad comes the foreign knowhow and knowledge itself. These come in varying forms and include knowledge about how a system works, how to operate it and develop its applications, and how to maintain it. All this is aimed at the western audience and when this technology is brought into Africa by the foreign forces, the existence of a certain amount of knowledge is assumed or taken for granted. Often this knowledge does not exist and users find it very difficult to relate this knowledge to their environment. The technology is, therefore, taken as being foreign and is consequently resisted.

One of the most important areas in which this problem is evident is in the education and training institutes. Most often than not, the syllabus used at such institutes is a replica of that offered by National Computing Centre (NCC), or Oxford or Cambridge universities in the UK. The training material and the syllabus is hardly adapted to the local needs or infrastructure of the country. The courses are highly technical and students are hardly taught about the social, cultural or organisational issues involved in computerisation. The textbooks used, where they exist, are all written abroad and are of little relevance or significance to the local environment. The theory taught bears no relation to what happens in practice (Odedra, 1990). The technology is, therefore, often taken as being alien.

Obviously, the reasons for the existing situation are far more complicated than those outlined above. Some of these issues are explained further in the next section, and so are the impact and implications of such forces on Africa and its society, and the reasons why such technology is enforced upon them in the first place.

10.3 Impact of such forces on Africa and its society

The impact of such forces on Africa have not always been those anticipated or intended; depending on the way the situation is analysed. Yes, the forces have introduced technology which would have otherwise taken a longer time to penetrate into Africa, largely due to the poor economic situation of the continent, but the overall result has been an increase in dependency on the advanced world. The main problem has been with the "foreignness" of this technology. The latter is introduced to a completely different culture; a culture which is not quite prepared to take advantage of the technology for various reasons.

It has to be remembered that technology is received differently in different cultural settings because it carries different social meanings in different settings. Attitudes towards the new technology from the lack of awareness or education, diversity of cultures and hierarchies, or departmental barriers in an organisation can all affect the successful introduction of technology. For any technology transfer process to be successful, the local ways of thinking and behaving must be taken into account. The system designed should not be divorced from its social environment as it is largely the organisational and social aspects which dampen the intended effect of technical innovations.

Due to the different social and cultural behaviour of the Africans, largely based on common perspectives, organisations function in a particular manner, and information technology is considered to be a threat to that system. Notions of rationality and efficiency differ as well as language, attitudes towards time and the meaning of authority. People are used to working with informal, non-standardised methods of data processing. The processes by which individuals make decisions in their work do not necessarily approximate to the rational ideal. Moreover, many of these countries have colonially inherited and often hardly changed economic, political, social and cultural structures, and corrupt and inefficient bureaucracies (Waema and Walsham, 1990). Such a structure is difficult to change, even with the use of IT.

In Africa, personnel recruitment in organisations occurs through personal influence (through relatives from the same tribe or village) and security of employment is considered a generally accepted norm. Rules about hiring and firing are rarely enforced. This often entails hiring a person with little management or technical skills for the wrong job. Often resources tied to specific purposes are diverted to meet urgent needs in other sectors. It is not unusual for special resources to be used for routine activities when the money is short. This can often affect important projects.

There is also a flexible attitude towards planning and scheduling. Plans are made and, quite often, laboriously documented. Paper commitments are, however, viewed as mirroring a certain situation in power relationships at one time but as these circumstances and relationships change, so will the urgency of carrying out mutually agreed actions. Organisations also tend to lack the capacity for organisational intelligence; the ability to learn from past mistakes is limited. The sad fact about African countries is that ignorance is an acceptable defence.

Decision-making remains personal to the managers; advice from those personnel with knowledge or experience about the technology is not sought. This affects many IT projects. Another problem is that large-scale organisations tend to be divided into departments and sub-departments controlled by individual top managers. Quite often, job descriptions of many of these managers do not exist but they may have secured the job anyhow. Moreover, the few specialists in some organisations tend to have 'generalist' ambitions, leaving the professional fields with junior and inexperienced people (Hyden, 1983).

All these above factors influence the way technology is accepted into African society. So far, the technology has been resisted by many as it is considered a threat to the existing system. As the use of technology would require some formalisation and adoption of unfamiliar techniques, the technology is viewed as an alien force brought in to break-up the system. Often, resistance is caused by the users as they do not know, and are not made aware of, the true capabilities of the technology. If the two parties involved in the process (the foreign forces and the national governments and organisations in Africa) took steps to increase computer literacy and awareness in these countries, then the situation could be salvaged.

The weak infrastructures in Africa, apart from the different socio-cultural attitudes, are also hindering the successful utilisation and application of information technology. Due to the poor economies, the education and training facilities are scarce, the telecommunications infrastructure poor, and government attitudes and policies relating to IT changing. Of these, it is the lack of education and training facilities and overall the lack of IT appreciation which has led to the current situation of lack of computer literacy and awareness in Africa and the one-way enforcement process by the foreign forces. This, together with the unsuccessful technology transfer, has resulted in minimal indigenous organisational capacity to use IT.

Apart from this, awareness of the value of information at both organisational and national level is lacking in Africa. The importance of the value of information is not yet appreciated by many people. Information, of vital importance to both the government and the organisations, is either lacking or is out of date. IT can make little impact if such data and information are lacking.

The existing weaknesses in Africa have perpetuated the dependency between African and industrialised countries. The foreign forces have taken advantage of the situation to increase dependency further. As these countries are predominantly buyers of IT and are proportionately more dependent on external sources of technical knowledge, there is no readily available solution to the implications of a one-way technology transfer apart from that of dependency. This technological dependency of some of these countries has been increasing since they do not possess adequate research, engineering and organisational capabilities to assimilate and adapt the technology to their own needs. Some of this dependency can be reduced with successful technology transfer but this again would depend on the local infrastructure and the perceived need for such information.

Apart from an increase in dependency, the overall impact of the foreign forces on Africa has been the acceptance of technology in a blindfolded manner, at both the national and organisational levels. There exists this notion that if the advanced countries use the technology and request us to do so as well, then we should. Few people in Africa have stopped to question the need for such technology and done anything about the foreign forces. This is largely because either the people have little power to do anything or the steps they take make little impact overall. It is only in the past three or four years that the Africans have started taking interest in the technology and questioned its need. Before that, it was a one-way process by the foreign forces. Little interest was shown in learning about this technology and making use of it for development. The poor economies, scarcity of foreign exchange and a number of national development priorities meant that IT received little attention.

Overall, in Africa, the problems are caused largely because of lack of computer literacy and awareness at the national level. The public sector installs computers because the international organisations have either donated the machines to them and they feel obliged to accept them, or they have insisted that the government start automating. The private sector started automating because the foreign companies started to do so; they feel they have to keep up with the trends.

Because of the manner in which the technology is acquired, usually without proper planning or questioning the real need for it, and because of the existing organisational structure described above, many of the systems installed fail and the equipment is often under-utilised. The foreignness of the technology, especially the software packages, further aggravates the problem as users often find it difficult to relate what they are expected to do to their own environment. The suppliers, who are largely in the money-making business, do not make things easier for the users either.

Where organisations genuinely want to make use of the technology, they are faced with the problem of lack of skilled personnel. Students who graduate from the few education and training institutions that exist in these countries often do not have the required skills, due to no fault of their own. These organisations are therefore forced to bring in personnel from abroad, increasing dependency further. The systems designed by these expatriates are largely alien to the local environment and the technology they transfer is minimal; resulting in further under-utilisation of equipment.

One may question the real need to transfer or impose this technology upon the developing world as, so far, it has only resulted in an increase in dependency of the developing world on the developed. The African countries, largely because of the influence of the "foreign forces", as well as IT/information systems professionals who are concerned about the development of these countries have come to believe and accept, either through experience or media hype, the fact that properly utilised computer systems can help organisations become more cost-effective in terms of financial, managerial and socio-economic resources. Moreover, they believe that IT can play an essential part in the process of development through economic growth. It is often suggested that if properly used in developing countries, IT can be the main factor in increasing productivity in public administration, the communications infrastructure, industry and agriculture (Dore, 1984; Ley, 1984; Dosa, 1985; Edmonds, 1986; Murphy, 1986; Gupta, 1987; etc.). This is further supported by the argument that the cost of IT is falling dramatically and that the systems based on them are becoming much easier to use and maintain.

In Africa, computers are still largely used for processing accounts, payroll, stock control, bills and statistics (Odedra, 1990); applications which are time-consuming if done manually. These applications have not contributed much to the overall development of these countries as either the information held is not used for decision-making or it is found to be of little significance to the overall development process. For the technology to be beneficial to the overall development of Africa, the choice of applications must match the development priorities set by government and have a high development impact. It has to be remembered that although the principles of IT are universal, the application of these principles are not. What the foreign forces and the Africans have done is to apply these principles to a completely different socio-cultural environment. This has led to an increase in dependency on the industrialised world and a waste of scarce foreign exchange. It has to be also remembered that IT is a mixed blessing and not a panacea. Not all problems of underdevelopment can be solved by IT. The majority of the population in Africa and other developing countries do not benefit from it. As Soupizet writes:

> *Computers don't clothe, don't cure, don't feed. Their power begins and ends with information. Their usefulness is therefore strictly linked to the effectiveness of the information ...* (Soupizet , 1987).

In summary, what has happened so far in Africa is that the foreign forces have continued over the years to bring the technology into a continent which has been, and still is, ill-prepared for the technology. The actions of the foreign forces could be for moral, commercial or other reasons but has led to an increase in dependency of Africa on the industrialised world. The African society, because of the way it is structured and because of the more pressing development priorities in their countries, has made little effort to improve its infrastructure, especially education and training, to cope with the technology or to integrate it into society. Overall, the technology is too foreign to the people of Africa. Together with the physical equipment comes the foreign knowhow and the expatriate consultants, neither of which they can relate to. Little effective technology transfer is taking place and overall, the situation is a little lopsided. There is a state of confusion amongst the society on how to integrate this foreign technology into their environment, which will still allow them to function in the way they have done in the past. Overall, the Africans themselves have done little to safeguard their interests with respect to IT.

10.4 Conclusion

So far, information technology has made little positive impact on Africa, largely because of the way the technology is introduced into these ill-prepared societies. Little computer literacy and awareness exists at the national level which has not only allowed foreign forces to take advantage of the situation but has led to an increase in dependency of the African nations on the industrialised countries. If manipulation by foreign forces is to be reduced and dependency decreased, the African nations themselves have to take steps; then the foreign forces have done their "bit". It may be too late and not advisable for the Africans to reject the technology override but with some effort from the Africans themselves, the situation can be salvaged.

One way to overcome some of these problems is to increase computer literacy and awareness in these countries. With more computer literacy and awareness, people may be in a better position to deal with suppliers, aid organisations, multinational organisations, and with the application of the technology itself. In other words, the role of the foreign forces and dependency can be reduced in such a manner.

For Africa to take advantage of this technology, urgent investments need to be made in education and training programmes; skilled personnel are vital not just for the successful utilisation of computers but for the general development of the nation. Both public and private sector organisations have to take steps towards achieving this. The luxury of under-utilised computer resources and perpetually increasing costs of questionable installations can no longer be tolerated.

Computer education and training facilities need to be both improved and increased and the number of places on existing computer courses expanded to cater for the new personnel required in the industry. The courses should cater not only for school-leavers but for people - including management - working in organisations which are to be computerised. Establishment of such facilities should be monitored either by a government computer committee or a computer society so that they meet agreed standards.

To achieve some of these goals, there may be a need to formulate a national IT education and training policy so that a level of computer awareness in general education can be achieved which will allow some of the population to have a sufficient degree of computer literacy to pursue the new technology and provide a pool of trained personnel sufficiently large to form a source of computer professionals. Any such policies formulated should later be integrated with the national IT policy.

Apart from training a pool of personnel for the industry, some education (and perhaps practical training) also needs to be given to government and other decision-makers about the new technology. New applications stand the risk of failure if they are not backed up by adequate efforts for education and awareness. The potential benefits of computers in information resource management depend heavily on the approach managers take towards their use.

The plans formulated should be both short and long term. The short-term plans should be to train IT professionals and the users, and to create a general awareness. The long-term plans should be determined by the Ministries of Education in each African state in accordance with the country's needs and should aim to achieve international standards.

The foreign domination in Africa can only be reduced with investment in computer education and training. Although Africa will never be in a position of being entirely independent, an increase in computer literacy and awareness may help it have a better stance against the foreign forces. The African governments themselves will need to invest in such programmes; it is of no interest to the foreign forces to do so for them.

References

Bennet, J. & Kalman, E. (1981) *Computing in Developing Nations*. North Holland, Amsterdam.

Botelho, A. J. J. (1992) *A Strategy for the Diffusion of Public Domain Software in Sub-Saharan Africa*, draft.

Brodman, J. Z. (1986) *Microcomputer Adoption in the Ministry of Finance and Planning, Kenya*, Development Discussion Paper no. 219, Harvard Institute for International Development, Cambridge, Mass.

Dore, R. (1984) Technological Self-reliance: Study ideal or self rhetoric. In: M. Fransman and K. King (eds) *Technological Capability in the Third World*, Macmillan Press, London.

Dosa, M. (1985) Information Technology Transfer as Technical Assistance for Development. *Journal of the American Society for Information Science*, **36** , 3.

Edmonds, L. (1986) *Information Technology, Public Administration and the Developing Countries*, paper presented at the Development Studies Association Conference, September.

Gupta, G. (1987) Role of Computer Technology in Developing Countries. *Information Technology for Development*, **2**, 1, March.

Hyden, G. (1983) *No Shortcuts to Progress: African Development Management in Perspective*. Heinemann.

Ley, C. (1984) Relations of Production and Technology. In: M. Fransman and K. King (eds) *Technological Capability in the Third World*. Macmillan Press, London.

Murphy, B. (1986) *The International Politics of Information Technology*. Croom Helm, London.

Odedra, M. (1990) *The Transfer of Information Technology to Developing Countries: Case Studies from Kenya, Zambia and Zimbabwe*. PhD thesis, London School of Economics.

Odedra, M. (1993) Does IT Aid Work?, forthcoming.

Rada, J. (1985) Information Technology and the Third World. In: J. Forrester (ed.) *The Information Technology Revolution*, Blackwell, UK.

Schware, R. & Trembour, A. (1985) Rethinking Microcomputer Technology Transfer to Third World Countries. *Science and Public Policy*, **12**, 1.

Soupizet, F. (1987) The Computer Tangle. *South*, July.

Tottle, G. & Down, D. (eds) (1983) *Computing for National Development*. Wiley.

Weama, T. & Walsham, G. (1990) Information Systems Strategy Formation in a Developing Country Bank: Implications for Technology Adoption Research Methodology. *Technological Forecasting and Social Change: An International Journal*.

11

Vincent Mosco

Whose New World Order?

11.1 Introduction

Social citizenship implies the development of a world order based on the principles of democratic participation and equality. These principles were embodied in the movement begun in the 1950s and led by the Non-aligned nations which called for a New World Economic Order and a New World Information and Communication Order. The Persian Gulf War gave us quite a different world order, one based on the principle of military supremacy. In order to create the global conditions for social citizenship we need to build on the former and recognise that the latter reflects little more than an empire in new clothes.

The Persian Gulf War gave us George Bush's version of a New World Order and resurrected Star Wars, the Strategic Defense Initiative Programme (SDI). This paper situates this New World Order in the context of a century of conflicts, dating from the development of the telegraph and deeply bound up with military considerations, over who would control the world communication and information order. These include the movement of the 1960s to 1980s that united non-aligned, mainly Third World, nations in the call for a New World Information and Communication Order (NWICO). Bush's New World Order, buttressed with a revived SDI, is just the latest turn in this history. But can the USA defend a new world order when it cannot maintain its own world economic power or maintain order within its own borders?

11.2 Background

Two of the more remarkable outcomes of the Persian Gulf War are the call for a New World Order and the rebirth of the "Star Wars" Strategic Defense Initiative (SDI) program. These developments are closely tied because SDI provides a military grounding for the USA version of a New Order.

The call for a New World Order is particularly striking for students of international communication and information policy issues. Since the 1950s, developing nations, formally organised in the Non-aligned Movement, forcefully pressed for a New World Order of their own. This became known as the New World Information and Communication Order (NWICO), itself an integral part of a New International Economic Order. These New Orders would provide for more equality and democracy in the production and distribution o f the world's resources, including mass media and information (Preston, Herman and Schiller, 1989). The call for a new order in communication culminated in 1979 with publication of the MacBride Commission Report, the product of a United Nations UNESCO commission, chaired by Nobel-laureate Sean MacBride and charged with identifying problems and proposing remedies.

The Commission was broadly based with representation from all regions of the world, including novelist Gabriel Garcia-Marquez and communication philosopher Marshall McLuhan. The Commission described how media and information systems in the developed world dominated flows of news and entertainment worldwide and called for a small start to address the problem by strengthening the mass media in the developing world (MacBride, 1984). One institutional product of the NWICO was the Intergovernmental Bureau for Informatics which aimed to provide the benefits of computer technology to the Third World (Mahoney, 1988).

The USA's response was to wage political warfare against this version of a New Order. As the book *Hope and Folly* demonstrates (Preston, Herman, and Schiller, 1989), the USA government and most major private media in the industrialised world attacked the report by distorting its recommendations. For example, western media repeatedly attacked a non-existent proposal to license journalists. The USA government, with the support of mainstream media, demanded the total rejection of the report's support for the principles of social citizenship. The USA denounced its calls for equity, balance, and democracy because any policies based on these principles would threaten the free marketplace of ideas, i.e. western controlled news, information, and data services. Supporters of the document responded by noting, among other things, that the overwhelming bias and distortion in the media's own coverage of the Commission showed how western media monopolies were increasingly able to choke off the flow of ideas that challenged their power. The USA and the UK gave the final thumbs down to reform by withdrawing from UNESCO, thereby leaving the organisation politically battered and with a much-reduced budget. By the time of the tenth anniversary of the Commission report, the *New York Times* ("Unesco Chief About to Face a Showdown", September 17, 1989) could safely declare that even the head of UNESCO was committed to ending what little remained of the New World Information and Communication Order, partly in order to coax back the USA and UK.

Why was the USA and some of its allies so overwhelmingly opposed to this New Order? The principal reason is that global mass media, from Hollywood films to NBC (now a subsidiary of one of the largest military providers in the world, General Electric) to Murdoch's News Corporation are big businesses and the major means to cement a dominant western view of the world. Any call for a New Order based on fairness, balance, equity and democracy, however slight, would threaten the existing mass media and information order.

Such a threat is potentially more significant than the nationalisation of a copper mine or a steel mill because the mass media produce ideas as well as a return on investment. And just as significantly, the USA communication order is bound up with the its global military hegemony.

11.3 The old order

The USA understood this very well because it had once been subjected to the domination of a world media order and spent much of the first half of this century overcoming it. In the latter part of the nineteenth century, international communication, largely telegraph and cable-based press wire services, were dominated by a cartel of European countries, principally the British Reuters, French Havas, and German Wolff (Smith, 1980). In language reminiscent of that used by many of today's developing nations, the USA, principally through the State Department and the Associated Press wire service, protested bitterly about European domination of the world's news and about how the image of America in the world was being filtered through European media.

Associated Press was especially upset that it could not strike deals with newspapers because the big European companies threatened retaliation. Its managing editor protested the "tenacious hold that a nineteenth century territorial allotment for news dissemination had upon the world." (Smith, 1980, p.44)

11.4 Building a USA order

The USA fought the European order on numerous fronts starting with what the government called its "chosen instrument", the Radio Corporation of America, the parent of NBC. The government established RCA by permitting General Electric, AT&T, Westinghouse, and United Fruit to pool their electronics patents and capital, giving the USA one big company to beat the Europeans by establishing global dominance in radio-based communication. Recognising the strategic significance of this decision, the USA government named a military representative to the RCA board and consistently made the company one of its top defence contractors. Today, as a subsidiary of General Electric, RCA is a major participant in the defence system.

In the 1960s, when communications satellite technology was ready for use, the USA established another "chosen instrument" to lead the world. The USA set up the Communications Satellite Corporation and the global Intelsat network, comprised of non-communist nations wishing to participate in international satellite communication. The USA managed the system for the world with an executive team filled with military and retired military officials (Kinsley, 1976), called Comsat an "old soldiers' home") who recognised the strategic significance of dominating the world communication order.

The developing nations call for their own New Order was therefore seen as a threat to USA strategic economic interests (the profits of global media companies), ideological interests (Western ideas like consumerism, individualism, private enterprise) and military interests (the links between big electronics firms and the war machine). The USA is now prepared to dispose of that threat once and for all by replacing the New Order that the developing world so desperately needs with its own version of a New Order, supported by the same form of military-backed enterprise that established USA domination in the first half of the twentieth century.

11.5 The Strategic Defence Initiative and the New Order

The Star Wars programme is central to the New Order. With its Patriot missiles and other "smart" weaponry (SDI is the largest computer research and development project in history) the USA revived the view that SDI could become a reality. As ex-President Bush told workers at the high-tech Raytheon company, manufacturer of the Patriot:

> *For years we've heard that antimissile defences won't work. The shooting down of a ballistic missile is impossible, like trying to hit a bullet with a bullet. Some people called it impossible; you called it your job. And they were wrong.* (*The Nation*, July 8, 1991, p.42)

Critics have been quick to point out that a few successful attacks on Scud missiles are hardly a test of a global defence against thousands of incoming intercontinental ballistic missiles. Moreover, they note that the Patriot was far from the efficient defence which the news media, dutifully transmitting Pentagon press releases, made it out to be. Most failed to hit their Scud targets. And whether or not they hit, more often than not they caused more damage than they were intended to prevent (*New York Times*, April 17, 1991: A11).

The critics are absolutely right, but, however necessary and well meaning, they miss a central point. SDI is not about a worldwide defence against nuclear weapons. It is not a global umbrella. As such, SDI cannot and will not work. Rather, SDI is about other matters which are more central to President Bush's New World Order and in these respects, SDI is already working. This helps to explain why in November 1991, despite the generally recognised end of the Cold War and the downfall of the Soviet Union, the USA government approved the largest annual funding for the SDI program and construction of a major anti-ballistic missile site.

First, SDI is working as an economic programme. It is a massive government investment of capital in USA multinational businesses. It represents the single largest computer communication research and development programme in history. It provides enormous financial benefits to companies like General Motors, which owns Hughes Aerospace and the major software firm Electronic Data Systems, and General Electric, the parent of RCA and NBC. Hence, despite the trendy rhetoric of laissez-faire, SDI is a programme of government assistance to its own transnational business.

Second, SDI is working politically. One of the tricky problems for national governments in an era of transnational business is ensuring that those businesses stay "on side", that they support national government policies as well as their own bottom line. The carrot of big research and development contracts is a major incentive to companies that take globalisation too seriously. Or as one Pentagon official put it when asked about IBM's apparent unwillingness to carry out research in areas that the Pentagon deems important: "Either IBM will decide that it will be good to do research in this field and to have a capability in it for defence in the 1990s or it will not. If it does not, there will be many others who will ... If IBM does not see that, then in my opinion their market share will decline." (Mosco, 1989, p.162)

Third, SDI is working as a system of beliefs, as an ideology that enshrines defence against the horrors of war as the principal driving force behind USA military strategy. According to this view, the Patriot missile and the accompanying Nintendo battlefield are symbols of a military committed to the clean, automated, morally justifiable goal of knocking offensive weapons out of the skies. The support for the USA's "defence" of Kuwait suggests that SDI may well be working in this respect as well.

Finally and most importantly, SDI is working militarily, but not as the high-tech defensive umbrella. SDI works as a loosely coupled set of military systems that enhance the ability to take offensive action against individual nations that are unwilling to accede to the New World Order. SDI is an ideological umbrella for a warfare system based on sophisticated electronics and massive fire power. As the Gulf War demonstrated, here too, it is working.

In essence, ex-President Bush's New Order is like many new and improved products in an age of advertising hype. It repackages old ideas about military domination and manifest destiny, only in a much more dangerous and destructive form. Nevertheless, even as Bush presents his New Order, cracks appear in the USA edifice. Europe and Japan represent formidable challenges. The USA's economy is stagnating under the weight of neglect, leaving its infrastructure crumbling, and crackpot policies like deregulating the banking system, leaving American taxpayers a bill for between one-half and one trillion dollars. The New Order and the renewed commitment to militarisation is an attack on America's poor - desperate for the commitment to social citizenship that would bring it much needed public housing, health care and education. In this respect, the USA could learn many lessons from the principles and proposals in the version of a New Order proposed by the developing world.

What would such an alternative order look like? According to Benjamin Mkapa, Tanzania's Minister of Information, rather than Bush's New World Order "based on the respect for the force of might", this would "herald more equal political, economic and cultural relations between states. It would promote greater sharing of productive technology and provide for more evenhanded competition. And it would open opportunities for all states and peoples, not just the developed ones, to express and enjoy a greater cultural freedom." (*New York Times*, June 5, 1991: A29) The west's own underdeveloped peoples are calling for nothing less than this full commitment to social citizenship.

References

Kinsley, Michael (1976) *Outer Space and Inner Sanctums.* Wiley Interscience, New York.

MacBride, Sean (1984) *Many Voices, One World, Report by the International Commission for the Study of Communication Problems.* UNESCO, New York.

Mahoney, Eileen (1988) The Intergovernmental Bureau for Informatics: An International Organization within the Changing World Political Economy. In: Vincent Mosco and Janet Wasko (eds) *The Political Economy of Information.* University of Wisconsin Press, Madison, pp.297-315.

Mosco, Vincent (1989) *The Pay-per Society: Computers and Communication in the Information Age.* Ablex, Norwood, N.J. and Garamond, Toronto.

Preston, William, Jr., Herman, Edward S. & Schiller, Herbert I. (1989) *Hope & Folly: The United States and Unesco 1945-1985.* University of Minnesota Press.

Smith, Anthony (1980) *The Geopolitics of Information.* Faber, London.

12

Diane Whitehouse

The summer school on 'Social citizenship in the information age': origins, highlights, and outcomes

12.1 Introduction

"This summer school is citizenship", announced Frances Morell of the Commission on Citizenship (UK) at the opening of the International Federation for Information Processing (IFIP) Working Group 9.2 first summer school. Located at the Falmer site of the Brighton Polytechnic in the south of England, the school was organised collaboratively by IFIP's Working Group 9.2 and by Brighton Polytechnic.

IFIP is an international federation of professional and technical organisations concerned with information processing, and the national groupings of these organisations, and has been in existence since 1960. The Federation is dedicated to improving worldwide communication and understanding among practioners of every nation about the role that information processing can play in all walks of life. The Federation has under its umbrella a range of different Technical Committees covering issues as diverse as programming, data communications, computer applications, systems modelling, education, and social issues. The brief of Technical Committee 9 (of which Working Group 9.2 is part) incorporates Computers and Society.

The group which organised the Brighton summer school is IFIP Working Group 9.2. This working group is concerned with Computers and Social Accountability. It was the first of five working groups subsumed under Technical Committee (TC) 9. The group has recently developed a tradition of day seminars, or what it calls 'Teach-Ins', which pre-empted the summer school. Since its formation in 1977, Working Group 9.2 has pursued a number of aims:

The aims of IFIP Working Group 9.2 are to:

(1) help make computer professionals, system designers and others aware of the social consequences of their work;

(2) develop criteria to determine how well the public is served when it comes into contact with computerised systems;

(3) enable and encourage designers and users of computer systems to make a human choice, that is, a choice which takes into account human needs and wishes.

Through the organisation of conferences, events such as the summer school, as well as the publication of scholarly books and articles, it puts these aims into effect (Berleur *et al.*, 1990; Yngstrom *et al.*, 1985).

IFIP is a regular organiser of conferences and workshops. It was helpful both in making an initial loan available to the summer school organisers, and in providing the group with a set of guidelines for conference organisation. All the members of WG9.2 were forthcoming in their enthusiasm and support for the proposed summer school; many contributed their ideas and suggestions on a regular basis, as well as their presence at the summer school. Brighton Polytechnic, and the Faculty of Information Technology in particular, was extremely generous in its financial and physical support for the school. Although IFIP, as a federation, had not previously organised a summer school, it now appears to have an interest in supporting the organisation of future summer schools as yet another form of academic and educational gathering and one which can particularly benefit the personal and professional formation of young informaticians[1] .

12.2 Origins of the summer school

At least once a year, the members of Working Group 9.2 meet in the university town of Namur, Belgium. Following the completion of the group's 'Landscapes'[2] conference in June 1988, several members of the group sat together over a farewell Sunday lunch. "What a great conference!" "Yes, it was good wasn't it. But it was a pity that there were so few younger participants. It would have been good to have more young people along." "Mmmm. I once went to something like that - a summer school." "Oh, really? What's that? A summer school?" From small acorns, large oak trees grow. From that lunchtime conversation developed a coherent proposal, a larger organising group, a location, dates, a financial plan, and much, much more.

The organising group consisted of Colin Beardon (University of Brighton, UK), Jan Holvast (Stichting Waakzaamheid Persoonsregistratie, The Netherlands), Felix van Rijn (Sociaal Wetenschappelijke Informatica, The

---

1 As an international grouping, Working Group 9.2 often uses the current European terminology in this field. For example, we may refer to information technology as informatics, and the personnel working within the informatics field as informaticians.

2 For further details on the 'Landscapes' conference, see the second of the two books produced by the working group (Berleur *et.al.*, 1990).

Netherlands), Diane Whitehouse (London Business School, UK), and Louise Yngstrom (Stockholm University, Sweden). All were involved in designing the conceptual framework of the school. Locally, a team from University of Brighton consisting of Tania Funston, Solveig Grover, Brenda Kelly-Evans and Richard Griffiths, was involved in getting the school physically off the ground. Both the international and the local organising groups met regularly; the former at the initial planning stages, and the latter over the duration of the final year. In all, the summer school took three years to come to fruition, though only the latter two of these required more active involvement. It was this close association and careful attention to planning which led to the school's success.

12.3 Aims and intentions of the summer school

The principal aim of the summer school was that all the participants would be introduced to both the theory and practice of social citizenship through the school's content and process; looking uniquely for an academic definition of social citizenship seemed to us to be searching in somewhat the wrong place. It was planned that the school would provide a week of intensive study and discussion, and that it would be interdisciplinary in character. We aimed for the school to encourage young people in particular to put forward their developing ideas in an informal, and supportive, setting.

The summer school was to strive for balanced excellence. It was intended to bring together some sixty young doctoral students, research assistants, and young academics alongside leading researchers in the field of informatics and society. It was resolved that, as far as possible, there would be an equal number of men and women involved at all levels within the summer school and that the school would attract participants from a wide range of cultural and national backgrounds. The attendance fee was kept as low as possible in order to enable participation from the widest possible community.

The summer school was further aided in its aims by the decision of Technical Committee 9 in July 1991 to establish an Affirmative Action policy. The group now aims to increase the participation of groups formerly under-represented by gender, region, and occupation in its working groups, task forces, conference committees and conference sessions. All the relevant chairpersons are actioned to make special efforts to seek and encourage suitable participants, and to report to the appropriate committees on their efforts to increase participation and the results achieved. It is this kind of policy which we feel will continue to encourage balanced excellence in all of Technical Committee 9's events.

Social citizenship concerns the rights and responsibilities of citizens and the relationship of these rights and responsibilities to questions of access, empowerment, and a sense of responsibility for the public good. It was of great concern to the organisers that not only would the school aim to explore and expand the conceptual framework underpinning the notion of social citizenship but that the organisation of the school would also be sufficiently flexible for the participants to experience social citizenship in the making. Hence, considerable emphasis was placed upon opportunity for involvement in both the structure and the process of the school. Far from looking for consensus, the group sought to create discussion, dialogue, and debate. The school explored a wide range of issues covering both how citizens and citizenship can benefit from the use of information technology, and how the technology can be made more responsive to the needs and concerns of citizens. The school covered all aspects of social citizenship concerned with informatics, whether at the individual, local, national, regional or global level.

12.4 Some highlights of the summer school

Exhorting the school's attendees to active involvement in social citizenship, Frances Morell of the UK Commission on Citizenship, opened the school. Frances Morell addressed over sixty partipants gathered together in a highly international grouping. Attendees came from as far afield as Kenya, Zaire, India, China, Japan, Austria, Sweden, Italy, Germany, Belgium, France, Mexico, Canada, the USA, as well as the UK. Participants came in the main from an informatics background, but also from disciplines as various as the social sciences, arts and humanities, and organisational studies. The school brought together both eminence and youth.

The days began with plenary session lectures given by noted contributors in the field, and the rest of the day consisted of a series of in-depth seminars, discussions, and workshops. Plenary sessions were addressed by Joe Weizenbaum (USA)[3], Vincent Mosco (Canada), Gunilla Bradley (Sweden), Jacques Berleur (Belgium), Romain Laufer (France), Klaus Brunnstein (Germany), and Frank Land, Richard Sizer and Satinder Gill (UK). Workshops and seminars, were led, amongst others, by Chrisanthi Avgerou (UK-Greece); Simone Fischer-Hübner (Germany); Tania Funston (UK); Paula Goossens (The Netherlands); Tom Mangan and Geoff Busby (UK); Peter Nilsson (Sweden); Jean-Louis Rigal (France); Peter Squires (UK); Rian Voet (The Netherlands); and Helen Watt (UK). Each of the plenary speakers also offered to run workshops, so that their audiences would gain from close questioning and further exploration of the concepts raised. Here, participants debated such topics as the concept of citizenship; access and empowerment through information technology; cultural diversity and informatics; overcoming disability; development, self-determination and information; human-centred approaches to information systems; and IT and the psychology of behaviour.

---

3 Appendix 1 contains a list of the presenters and topics of the various plenary sessions and workshops that were held during the week of the School. Each list is presented in alphabetic order of name.

Some 40 per cent of the participants were women, a rather more even balance than at many information technology-related events. Registered students constituted 25 per cent of the participants and, amongst the rest, there was a heterogeneous mix of younger academic staff and established scholars. The school therefore provided the opportunity to sit at the feet of well-known and established scholars, and free and frank discussion arose as a result. The number of attendees was ideal in terms of enabling participants to form quickly an excellent *esprit de corps*. The site, although it provided easy access to both Brighton and Lewes, was nevertheless reasonably isolated which was useful in helping to maintain continuity.

Despite gloriously sunny, hot August weather, on none of the weekday afternoons did conference attendees skip off elsewhere to shop and sightsee, a mark of considerable commitment to the event. Animated discussion groups were to be found scattered throughout the polytechnic campus debating, for example, how can developing countries become more than passive receivers of information technology? How can women enter the information technology profession in significant numbers? What impact has information technology had on people with disabilities and what part can it play in integrating more severely disabled people into society? In what ways can information systems be made less technically vulnerable and how can society become less vulnerable to information technology?

Of constant debate were the questions, what precisely is meant by both "citizenship" and "social citizenship"? Although the issue is firmly on the British political and social agenda (the summer school skilfully took place the week after the 1991 Government's announcement of its Citizen's Charter and is a topic being debated by all three of the main political parties), citizenship has very different meanings for people of different political, ideological, and cultural orientations. A consideration of the notion of social citizenship is one which is particularly appropriate to the challenges of the information age; whether we mean by this civil, political, economic, or social rights and responsibilities. In an increasingly global society, what meaning do these issues have for citizens in Asia, Africa, Latin America, North America, and other regions of Europe, for example? Sitting around a lunchtime table, it was not uncommon to catch, for example, a West African, Japanese, Swede, and Briton sitting together, and to hear the question: "What does citizenship mean to people in your country?" It is hoped that the forms of interaction begun during this August week will lead to continued and fruitful contact between the participants in years to come. One of the challenges of the school was not simply to absorb passively received wisdom but to examine critically the concepts introduced. To this extent, there was considerable questioning of the functionalism of contemporary informatics educational curricula in terms of their preparation of citizens for the workforce, not necessarily for a wider social experience.

Each day culminated in a live theatre performance, a production of the "Court of Ethics". This Swiss play, consisting of five acts, has been specifically designed to involve both actors and audience in the mock trial of a systems analyst accused of social irresponsibility (Tritt, undated). The voice-activated vacuum cleaner designed by the analyst runs amok and terrorises household pets whilst children use it to play slalom in underground carparks. The "analyst for the week", Peter Nilsson of Sweden, and the various prosecutors and court officials succeeded in achieving intense active involvement from the jury (that is, the audience). The play was very successful in raising many important issues relating to social responsibility, as well as being sheer good fun. In the corridors, over coffee, in the bar, throughout the week there was animated debate about the relative guilt or innocence of the analyst and of the various software and design companies involved in the project. At one point in time, so heated was the discussion, it seemed as though the court itself would be overrun by a revolutionary jury! In this context, it is noteworthy that the use of drama in informatics teaching is becoming an area of increasing interest to researchers, academics, and educationalists (Smithson & Hirschheim, 1992).

Several afternoons came to a close with a Speaker's Corner event, a gathering akin to the sights and sounds of London's Hyde Park each Sunday morning. Here, the presenters of seminars and other individuals with issues to raise, were able to talk to a more general public about the outcomes of their sessions, and other questions. Small groups met in the location of the main conference hall to share with each other the experiences and debates of their particular session. In addition, many other interactive activities were built into the week's programme.

The social programme gave the school's participants a very real impression of working hard and playing hard. The balance between intensive hard work in the halls and classrooms during the working day and the focused, but equally stimulating, social events of the evening was carefully chosen and proved to be an immense success. Discussions continued, and we scarcely knew where work ended and leisure began.

The Banqueting Hall of Brighton's Regency Pavilion was the site for an entertaining welcoming address by the Mayor of Brighton, Councillor Joseph Townsend. As a former researcher at the University of Sussex's Science Policy Research Unit, Cllr Townsend was keenly aware of the potential impact of contemporary technologies upon social citizenship, as they facilitate communications and meanwhile encroach upon individual and group freedoms. He advocated our experiencing social citizenship in a rather more immediate fashion through the cultural and social delights of the municipality. The school's contingent wandered off through paths trod formerly by generations of Anglo-Saxons, Romans, and Neolithic tribespeople. There we discovered the various contemporary gastronomic establishments of Brighton's Regency Lanes.

A former Labour Party Leader, the Right Honourable Michael Foot, in his guise as President of the Thomas Paine Society, delivered to the school a highly informative lecture on the life of the author of *The Age of Reason* and

Rights of Man (Paine, 1969). The school's participants and invited friends and colleagues sat in the very room at the White Hart Hotel in Lewes, near Brighton, where Paine and his fellow citizens had gathered. Mr Foot's passionate rendition of the themes of independence and autonomy that Paine had taken up in his tracts supporting the American Declaration of Independence (1776) and the French Revolution (1789) provided a fitting culmination for the week's endeavours.

On a lighter note, a local folk band invited us to a strenuous evening of English traditional dances in a local village hall. The school was not only intellectually, but also physically, invigorating.

Comments from the school's participants assessing the week's experiences have included the following: "It was the best organised, most inspiring meeting I've attended - and excellent fun to boot."; "The flavour of the school was excellent."; "It was very well balanced."; "It works!"; "It was the best event I have ever been to and I met some immensely stimulating people."; "It was like doing another masters degree all over again, but intensely, in a single week."

12.5 Outcomes of the summer school

Whilst the feedback from the event indicates that it was enjoyed by all and that there was a successful sharing of knowledge, there are a number of weaknesses that were evident in the school's programme. There were some problems with publicity. Some school participants were not able to stay for the whole of the week, and this led to the last day of the school being somewhat overloaded with plenary sessions. The event was not formally underwritten. Whilst it had been decided that all participants should pay their own way in order to keep down the cost for student attendees, this policy led to a number of difficulties with potential speakers.

There are, however, several positive outcomes of the summer school. These include a plan to organise further summer schools, a student-centred electronic network, a video version of the summer school play, and a publication.

The next summer school is currently being planned for The Netherlands in the summer of 1994. On the organising committee are a number of the organisers from the first school as well as student representatives from the Brighton event. Whilst its exact theme has not yet been fixed, it is anticipated that the school will continue to promote the general agenda of Working Group 9.2 which covers such topics as computers and social accountability, information technology and the distribution of wealth, the culture of the artificial as manifested in computer technology, vulnerability and risk in the information age, and opportunities for action.

A young people's informatics network is currently being organised by a small group of students who attended the summer school. Over a dozen of the young researchers from four separate countries present at the school aim to keep informed of each other's research work. As they describe it: "While riding the train (and the Jetfoil, and the train...) from Brighton to Namur, we couldn't help but to talk in positive terms about the week's experiences. The plenary sessions, workshops, and informal discussions brought into focus many aspects of information technology for us, insights which we find both personally and professionally valuable. May we guess that you feel the same?[4]"

By the end of August 1991, they had formed an electronic network that enables them to send each other relevant articles, conference/colloquium information, or general "updates". In an increasingly global society, we believe that it is increasingly important for networks of researchers to talk to each other in this way; these young researchers are starting the habit early.

Two of the school's other participants, Felix van Rijn (The Netherlands) and David Pullinger (Scotland), are associated with a proposal to put together a video version of the play, 'Court of Ethics'. There is no further news as yet.

Various papers presented at the school and ideas developed during the course of the summer school are gathered together in this collection of papers under the title of "Social citizenship in the information age". It is intended that the papers will stimulate debate and discussion as lively as that which took place during the summer school week. It is anticipated that it will be useful in helping people like the summer school participants, young academics and researchers, to set up new courses and new research examining issues relating to computers and society and, more specifically, the issues of social citizenship. It is particularly intended to act as a supporting textbook for educationalists and trainers wishing to put on a course or curriculum which raises social citizenship issues as a part or as a whole of what it intends to do.

Finally, since it is difficult to transfer to paper the precise sense of optimism, collaboration, and dynamism, that characterised the entire week of the summer school, the only real response for those interested is to experience the next one!

For further details on IFIP WG9.2's past and future activities, contact:

Professor Jacques Berleur
Chairperson
IFIP WG9.2
Institut d'Informatique
Facultes Universitaires Notre Dame de la Paix (FUNDP)
Rue de Bruxelles 61
5000 Namur
Belgium

---

4 Letter dated 23 August, 1991, from Patrick Gobin, Kathleen Gregg, and Benoit Kusters of the University of Namur, Belgium, to other young researchers attending the Summer School.

References

Berleur, J., Clement,A. , Sizer, R. & Whitehouse, D. (1990) *The Information Society: Evolving Landscapes.* New York & North York (Canada): Springer Verlag & Captus University Publications.

Paine, T. (1969) *Rights of Man.* London: Penguin Books.

Smithson, S. & Hirschheim, R. (1992) Information systems teaching: a debate on the user-system interface in end-user computing. *Journal of Information Systems.* **2** , 1, pp. 61-78.

Tritt, G. (undated) Copies of the play are available from Graham Tritt, PO Box 302, 3000 Berne 25, Switzerland.

Yngstrom, L, Sizer, R., Berleur, J. & Laufer, R. (1985) *Can Information Technology Result in Benevolent Bureaucracy?* Amsterdam: Elsevier Science Publishers BV.